The First Fifty

A Biographical History of
SEASIDE HEIGHTS, NEW JERSEY

By
C. Byron Wortman

Edited By
George Zuckerman

1963

Publication Sponsored by
50th Anniversary Committee

"THE FIRST FIFTY"

A Biographical History of
SEASIDE HEIGHTS, N. J.

By
C. BYRON WORTMAN

Permanently encrusted with salt and sunburn from a half century of living within sound of the Atlantic Ocean's splashing surf, the author found a close kinship with the people and the place with which these pages deal. A New York newspaper man for many years, he has never forsaken the environs of his Native Jersey Shore as a home, despite the opportunity to compare it with other climes. If anything, travel has only served to strengthen his conviction that the Jersey Coast has no equal. Therefore, if the writing should show a flavor of prejudice in that direction, it should be forgiven.

Edited by
GEORGE ZUCKERMAN

Active in affairs of New Jersey's Resorts for the years
it took to turn his remaining hair a respectable tint of
grey, the Editor has written for leading publications and
news syndicates. His writings include comments on for-
eign resorts and travel. During the past 25 years he has
come to know well, the leading figure in this volume—
the folks associated with him—and to acquire a true appreciation of the ingenuity and imagination which went
into making Seaside Heights a dynamic resort, attract-
ing growing thousands of people, and contributing sub-
stantially to the economic growth of the county and
State.

ACKNOWLEDGMENTS

The Author and Editor extend sincere appreciation to the following people, and to all others who made available material which helped in the preparation of this book. (Listed alphabetically.)

Florian Beiseigel
George Bennett
Vernon Casler
Mrs. Louise Gilmore
Edward F. Groffie
Mrs. Virginia Groffie
Mrs. Miriam Harding
Preston Hibbler
Mrs. Phoebe Hiering
William Hiering
Mrs. Frances Hopson
Mrs. Mary Kramer
Joseph P. McDevitt
William Polhemus
Harry Smith
Joseph W. Spangenberg
W. Patrick Tunney
Kenneth C. Wynne, Jr.

Contents

Chapter   *Page*

1. A Town is Born 1
2. Man of Action 5
3. Opening the Way 9
4. The Hard Road Up 14
5. Fire, Storm and War 19
6. The Hiering Heritage 22
7. The Bridge to Triumph 27
8. Growing Pains 31
9. A World of Fun 37
10. Safety on the Beaches 41
11. Protection and Service 45
12. Tribute to God 50
13. The Red-Haired Pirate 54
14. Things Just Don't Happen 59
15. Our People 62

Airview showing the Boro's expanse between Barnegat Bay and the Ocean, with Funtown USA and its great variety of amusements projecting seaward from the Boardwalk (lower left) and the Casino Pier and Venice Arcade (upper right). The famous beaches attract countless thousands each year and are among the most popular along the entire coast.

Mayor J. Stanley Tunney

Councilman William C. Ambrunn

Councilman Thomas R. Reutter

Councilman Hugh A. McDevitt

Councilman David J. P. Bentz

Councilman John C. Snow

Councilman Frank L. Walker

At "Funtown" entrance stand Police Chief Joseph McDevitt and Lt. Edward Groffie.

At "Casino" are Kenneth Wynne, Jr., Managing Director and John FitzGerald, its widely known president.

Greatest concentration of amusements and focal points of Boardwalk are "Funtown USA" and the "Casino". Keeping watchful eye over safety of millions of bathers on broad, white beaches are Seaside Heights Beach Patrol Boat, maintained by the Boro, and N.J. State helicopter which makes periodic inspections.

1 ◆

A Town is Born

The development and growth of the American community has taken many forms. But the principal ingredient of this great phenomenon has always been, the indomitable spirit of the men and women whose determination and vision make it so.

There is no true model from which to seek guidance. Each has its own peculiar geographic locations and contours; each its particular set of natural resources.

This is the story of one such town; a good town; Seaside Heights, on the Atlantic Coast of New Jersey.

All other considerations aside, listen to these words spoken 50 years apart by two men who played leading roles in its history.

Mayor Edmund C. Kramer, in 1913, replying to a complaint that speeding autos were endangering lives of residents of the infant borough:

"I did not think there was anyone in Seaside Heights who had time enough to spare to see this speeding. There is no one in Seaside Heights who is so slow as to be hit by a motor car."

Mayor J. Stanley Tunney, a half century later in 1963, replying to an observation that Seaside Heights, "is one of the finest seashore resorts in New Jersey."

"There are *two* words that don't belong in that description: they are "one of." This IS the finest! And don't get the idea we're resting on the oars. Just wait and see what happens in the years ahead!"

These may not be words that future historians will write in indelible ink, but they bespeak the determination and the impatience with delay that marked the community growth.

These were the characteristics that helped Seaside Heights emerge from barren sand dunes and scrub vegetation, inhabited mainly by seagulls, into a mecca for thousands who annually shed their work-a-day cares under the soothing influence of its God-given and man-made attractions.

There were trials and errors, triumphs and setbacks, failures and successes, all the growing pains that are part of maturity. But never, was there doubt! Never doubt, but that some day from the rawness would flower a community that would be a source of pride to its own people and inspiration to those who will build the future.

There are many names along with those of Mayor Kramer and Mayor Tunney sprinkled across the records that document the growth of Seaside Heights. Such names as Hiering, Cummings, Goodwin, Marcy, Sayles, Lawyer, Boyd, McDevitt, Freeman. Some have passed into antiquity. But many still flourish, nourished by roots put down a half century ago.

What is Seaside Heights? Physically, it is an area that encompasses less than one square mile on the Barnegat peninsular coast of New Jersey's Ocean County. The restless Atlantic washes its beaches on the east. Historic Barnegat Bay hems it in on the west.

Its northern neighbor is the Ortley Beach section of Dover Township. On the south lies Seaside Park, whose economic well-being is closely linked with it. Excellent highway and bridge facilities make Seaside Heights easily accessible within easy rides of the great metropolitan centers of Philadelphia, New York and northern New Jersey.

As the permanent home of some 1000 year-around residents, it contains the most modern of municipal facilities. Good schools educate its youth; churches of many faiths fulfill the spiritual needs. Service and community organizations cater to cultural appetites.

The police department under Chief Joseph McDevitt and Lt. Edward Groffie is equipped better than most major cities. So is the fine volunteer fire department under Chief "Del" Hopson that sprang into being back in the days when men pulled by hand the first crude equipment.

That, partially describes Seaside Heights as a town. But it is far from the whole story. That story can only be told when Seaside Heights is put in its true perspective as a resort: as the gem in a necklace of sanctuaries of vacation pleasure that dot the New Jersey coast.

When winter is done and summer comes, the town becomes a vibrant host; a pulsating playground for all ages: joyous, fun-seeking youth; happy honeymooners, carefree family groups. It is a place where vacation dreams come true for growing thousands each year.

They come for a day, a week, a month, a season, and find in bountiful measure facilities to satisfy their needs and tastes. As many as 70,000 a day have been drawn, as if by a giant magnet, to savor the wealth of activities the town has to offer.

There is swimming from sparkling white sandy beaches in the wave-crested Atlantic Ocean or the shimmering waters of the Barnegat. For the less venturesome there are huge pools.

Fishing abounds, whether it be deep-sea or surf-casting in the ocean or lazy drifting on the quiet bay. There is boating of every style and water-skiing; there are tennis and bicycling; theaters and dancing. Hotels, motels and guest cottages offer shelter and good restaurants satisfy the inner man.

Towering over all, however, is the great boardwalk amusement center. Here, without challenge, Seaside Heights can claim the greatest concentration of games and amusement rides in the world. Ablaze with lights in myriad colors the boardwalk at night has all the ingredients of mardi gras.

How did all this come to pass? How long has it been thus? Did someone wave a giant magic wand and produce it all in one flashing moment? The answer, of course, is no.

The evolution of a resort such as Seaside Heights has little touch of the miracle. Stretching back over a half century there is a long and rocky trail, uncharted at the beginning and beset by pitfalls and obstacles all along its course. Some of these were man-made; some were nature's, as though to warn that success does not come easily. Resting beside the blue Atlantic, the town has drawn heavily upon the great benefits it has to offer. Generously it has presented its zestful waters to revitalize the weary; yielded up food fish and sport; cooled the breezes to temper searing summer heat. Then it has been a gentle and obedient servant.

But time and again, as though exacting some payment for what it has given, the ocean became a raging monster. Like a headstrong child smashing his toys, the great sea has hurled itself against the shore, battering man's structures, in uncontrollable fury.

Fire and hurricane winds have added to nature's exacting toll. But always from the wreckage, the people have salvaged, cleared away and built anew. Always with an eye to the future!

The town survived a great depression, during which it came dangerously close to financial ruin, with its only bank closed never to reopen.

An honor roll is mute testimony to the men it gave to help the nation fight three wars.

These indeed, "were the times that try men's souls." But happily, Seaside Heights has never been without men who thrive on adversity, as well as success.

Never, since the days when the Manhasset Realty Company was first formed by a group of Camden and Philadelphia residents to breathe life into the community has Seaside Heights wanted for leadership.

That was in 1909. Four years were to pass before, under legislative action, it would become an incorporated borough.

In those early days a 40 foot beachfront lot could be purchased for $100. Today a plot of similar size commands a price as high as $50,000. And with multiplied land values has come, too, a multiplication of appreciation of those who bore the responsibility and the problems.

Along with their determination, their impatience of delay and their vision, there was also a vast humility that stands as a beacon for those to follow.

Hark to the words of Mayor Tunney:

"I have spent more than half of my 77 years here. Every morning when I get up, I look out to sea and I figure I'm looking God right in the face. And I thank Him for not only His goodness, but for His help in letting me play a part in creating this community."

2 ◆

Man of Action

Joseph Stanley Tunney has been mayor of Seaside Heights for almost a quarter of a century. There are many facets to the character of this man but none shine through more than his single-minded purpose, his firm conviction, that there is no place like his town.

Whatever activity may engage him in his energetic 77th year, and his interests are many, the end result is certain to bear upon the continued growth and development of Seaside Heights.

With typical directness, he considers that his entrance into political life of the borough was forced upon him rather than motivated by any desire for personal glorification. Then as now, he was fighting for improvements in resort facilities. But he freely confesses that there was a certain amount of personal economics involved.

It was in the late 20's and he had just made his first faltering steps into business. He, his late wife, Louise, and their six children, were laboring to breathe a spark of economic solvency into a small restaurant business on a beachfront pier. His assets, at the outset, he recalls, consisted of "one 15-cent oyster knife," plus an overpowering determination that he had inherited in full measure from his Irish ancestors.

But borough officials of that day considered the pier unsafe. One Sunday afternoon they sent police to close the Tunney business.

"They put a rope across the front to keep people out," he relates. "So, I cut the rope."

His next stop was a cell in the borough jail. His wife attempted to continue operating the business. But she, too, was taken into custody. Then their eldest daughter, Frances, took over, with other young Tunneys waiting in reserve.

Eventually officials relented. He and his wife were released and the charges dropped. But the incident, with all its comic aspects, was to have a lasting effect. It shaped the history of the town.

Smoldering under the indignity of his arrest, he determined then and there that the municipal government needed a change and that he was the man to bring it about.

But it wasn't easy and it didn't happen quickly.

"I began attending every council meeting and when something was done that I thought was not right, I got up on my two feet and said so."

He began to attract the public's attention, but he also attracted a shadow!

"At every council meeting the Mayor (the late Charles Smith) would order a cop to sit beside me. Joe McDevitt, our present police chief got the job. He never had to remove me physically from a meeting, but believe me I received many invitations to leave."

It was 1935 before "Stan" Tunney made his first bid as a candidate for office. And lost. But he returned to the battle the next year and led his ticket to win his first seat on council.

It was at a time when the borough was indeed feeling its growing pains. The scars of the depression were beginning to disappear and Seaside Heights was growing.

There had been a 35 percent increase in building—beachfront buildings, homes and business structures all over town. There was internal friction over local policies—whether to build an electric generating plant; how to regulate business.

Mr. Tunney was against the power project. Anything that would help the beachfront flourish, he was for. He evidently was right in both respects. In 1939 he became a candidate for mayor, running against Acting Mayor Edward J. Ryan, and squeaked through to victory.

"It was a close election and I just got under the wire," he recalls. But his views on Seaside Heights and its future were beginning to mold solid support. He faced some opposition when he ran for reelection in 1941 and in 1943, but since that time there has been no real contest for the mayoralty.

"They're just waiting for me to die, I guess," Mayor Tunney says.

With him on council for most of the last two decades have been Councilmen Frank Walker, Thomas Ruetter, Hugh McDevitt, William C. Ambrunn, David J. P. Bentz and John Snow, men who have helped in shaping the destiny of the resort.

In that time the course of borough business has flowed smoothly. Many improvements have been made and, of course, some problems have arisen. But at no time has there been any serious internal controversy to shatter the harmony that has accompanied Seaside Heights' constant progress.

It was only natural, then, that in such an atmosphere Mayor Tunney turned his attention to some of the external situations that he considered obstacles for his community's betterment.

This gave him a wider field in which to range and fight for his town.

A colorful personality has provided a perfect foil for the mental and physical energies that seem to spring from a bottomless well. Slight of build, he has a deeply-tanned, weather-beaten face, the marks of years spent in the open. There's a friendly twinkle in his eyes and an unruly shock of white hair lends height to his nature.

Only in battle does that twinkle in his eyes turn to sparks. Then, too, his language can get as salty as the white-crested ocean combers that endlessly pound the beach at his door.

This is all part of the make-up of a man who had to fight every inch of the way for survival, personally and publicly. As a youngster he had little time for formal education. So he did the next best thing. He built upon experience—the good and the bad.

Naturally, his personal fortunes have flourished with those of his community. His native instinct for business has served him well. The phrase "a self-made man" has grown worn and trite with over-use. But it's a cloak that Mayor Tunney wears well, graciously and without false modesty.

That "15-cent oyster knife," has been parlayed into vast business and real estate interests.

Mayor Tunney's personal and official activities have brought him into contact with a great number of people far beyond the narrow confines of his home town. Many of these contacts have developed into deep friendships. Some have naturally led to something less as he pursued his Barnum-like super-salesman role in the interest of Seaside Heights.

But whichever way the chips have fallen—and they generally fly thick and fast wherever he is at work—there has always remained for him a deep respect, whether it be friend or foe.

This stems largely from being loyal in his friendships, personal and political, and his ingrained habit of never hesitating to speak his mind on any subject relating to the welfare of his town. Indirection is not his method. He says what he thinks and he means what he says! So there is no room for doubt in anyone's mind about his intentions. And when he tackles a problem—and he never seems to rest when there is something to be accomplished—the chances are good that it will eventually be resolved in his—meaning Seaside Heights'—favor.

There have been many matters that have kept him on the go constantly during the last decade. Some have been settled to his satisfaction. Some are still presenting a challenge. And some are stored in the back of his mind for future action.

Christian Hiering

A pioneer resident; his heritage has left a strong influence on the community.

Edmund C. Kramer

first Mayor, being honored during the 50th Anniversary celebration.

Minutes of first Meeting of Incorporators
of
Manhasset Realty Company

A meeting of the incorporators of the Manhasset Realty Company was held at No. 227 Market Street, Camden, New Jersey, designated in the certificate of incorporation as the location of the principal office of the company in New Jersey, on the twenty seventh day of January, A. D. 1909, at three o'clock in the afternoon, pursuant to a written waiver of notice signed by all of the incorporators, fixing the time and place aforesaid.

All of the incorporators were present in person, namely: Walter J. Frosscup, George C Frosscup, Allen H Frosscup.

On motion Mr. Allen H Frosscup was appointed chairman and Mr. Walter J Frosscup was appointed Secretary of the meeting.

The chairman reported that the certificate of incorporation of the company was recorded in the Clerk's office of the County of Camden, on the twenty fifth day of January, A D 1909, in Book No. 36 of Corporations, page 379 etc., and was filed and recorded in the office of Secretary of State on the twenty sixth day of January, in the year one thousand nine hundred and nine, and presented a certified copy of said certificate of incorporation.

The Secretary presented and read a waiver of notice of this meeting

The Secretary presented a form of By-laws for the regulation of the affairs of the company which were unanimously adopted.

H E Davis and S C Archer were appointed inspect

In classic penmanship of the day. ... The first minutes of the Manhasset Realty Co., drawn in 1909, which gave life to the new community.

Some of the town's leading citizens when they were somewhat younger . . . and had more hair.

The first Life Saving crew stationed along this section . . . forerunner of the present day Coast Guard.

Early means of transport, the donkey trolley which ran into the area from the north.

Primitive fire equipment marked the early volunteer days.

The Freeman Carousel, forerunner of the huge present day amusement industry which is the backbone of the Boro's economy. ▼

20681

3 ◆

Opening the Way

One of the major problems from which he never turns, is the accessibility of Seaside Heights to the growing thousands of people who want to come here.

In its infancy the town could be reached by railroad principally. Today it can be reached only by automobile or boat. The attraction of more people, means more cars and more cars mean traffic congestion. And traffic tieups have a discouraging effect on would-be visitors.

This is something that the Mayor cannot abide. Thus he has spent the last 15 years in a major campaign for good access roads. The evidence is plain that he has made significant gains —but he still is not satisfied.

For many decades Seaside Heights and its neighboring communities, Seaside Park and Lavallette were served only by narrow wooden bridges over Barnegat Bay. They were uncomfortable to ride over, costly to maintain and far too narrow to handle the growing motor vehicle traffic.

It took long years of pounding on doors at the State House in Trenton and persuasive talking into political ears before Mayor Tunney and other resort officials affected could convince highway officials that wooden bridges had gone out of style.

But the mayor is a convincing talker. So in 1950 a new concrete and steel structure was finally strung across the barrier waters. The majestic $6,000,000 Thomas A. Mathis Bridge, named for Ocean County's long-time Republican political leader, was a beautiful sight to see and a major improvement in traffic conditions. But it reached only as far as Pelican Island to the west of Seaside Heights. So, Mayor Tunney returned to the wars. Now there is a six-lane bridge and approach network that moves traffic easily into the resort area.

That, would seem to be that! But it isn't! The new bridge complex is fine. And so is the Garden State Parkway, that speeds summer visitors to the shore areas.

But there is a seven-mile stretch of Route 37 from the Parkway to the bridge that looms as a menacing red ribbon so far as Mayor Tunney is concerned. Its constricting influence on traffic builds up into aggravating delays for summer visitors.

Mayor Tunney wants the route converted into a dual highway from the Parkway to the bridge. Then and only then, will he be satisfied. For the moment, at least.

What methods does he employ to influence people beyond Seaside's borders to his point of view? He sells. He campaigns. He crusades. With banners waving!

There was the time when the Parkway was first proposed and opposition to it developed because some thought the cost would be prohibitive. Largely instrumental in overcoming the opposition and the eventual successful referendum of approval was an education program carried on throughout the state to acquaint the people with the facts. Pioneering in the campaign was the New Jersey Resort Association, of which Mayor Tunney is a past President. The organization put up among the first sizeable cash contributions toward the fund that was raised to finance the program of education.

One of Mayor Tunney's closest allies in projects of this progressive nature is Ocean County Freeholder A. Paul King. Like the mayor, Freeholder Paul King is also a past president of the State Resort Association. A close personal friendship based on mutual respect, has built up between the two as they fought side by side to solve not only the highway problem but such ever-present problems as beach erosion, etc., always prime factors in resort life. Ocean County's State Senator W. Steelman

Mathis, son of the late Thomas A. Mathis, is another who works closely with Mayor Tunney.

Now they are working toward a goal of staggering import to entire Ocean County: establishment of a Pinelands Jetport in the Ocean-Burlington County area. They envision a completely new era if the project should materialize, with recreational and industrial facilities developing to undreamed of proportions.

The economy of Seaside Heights is dependent largely on the attraction of people to its amusement facilities, including the boardwalk games. Its economy affects the wide segment of Ocean County which surrounds it.

Mayor Tunney never fought harder than he did four years ago when the legality of the boardwalk games was under fire and the very life blood of the beachfront was threatened.

The mayor is, and always was, president of the New Jersey Amusement Board of Trade, an organization of amusement business people who operate most of the game-type concessions.

Under his leadership, the organization sponsored the 1959 referendum which led to the legalization of boardwalk and amusement park games.

The state-wide referendum was carried by the largest majority of any in recent N.J. history, supported in counties in which such types of business do not even exist! According to veteran political observers, its success was due largely to the fact that "Stan" Tunney made a personal appeal to everyone of the 550 mayors in the State of New Jersey, telling them of the problem that existed for resort areas and enlisting their support. The response at the polls was overwhelming.

Just how deeply he felt about the matter—and how well he transmitted his feelings to others—is easily explained in this statement he made at the time.

"You're damn'd right, I have some gripes. I'm plenty good and mad about this business of boardwalk concessionaires being continually badgered with charges of operating gambling places." "When a kid busts a balloon, that takes skill. When a man correctly guesses someone's weight, that takes skill. When a fellow manages to knock down a stack of wooden milk bottles —well, that sure as heck takes skill, and if you don't think so, try it sometime."

"New Jersey legalizes race tracks where a man can lose his

shirt and often does. What, I'd like to know, is so wrong about letting the working man and his family win a pound of bacon, a doll, or a carton of cigarettes?"

He predicted that the referendum would end this "nonsense" and that it would pass five-to-one in favor of "giving the little man a chance to play." The results prove how right he was!

The "little" man has always played a principal role in Mayor Tunney's planning of resort facilities. He believes firmly that the working man with limited income deserves a place to bring his family when the hot breath of summer sears the inland areas.

One method of translating that thinking into action has been the practice of keeping access costs to natural assets of the borough, such as the beaches, at a minimum.

"We charge 10 cents a day for the use of the beach except on Sunday, when it's only 25 cents," Mayor Tunney says. "And we don't make any charge for children under 12. The purpose of this is to give everyone a chance to help pay for keeping the beach clean and for protection by lifeguards and beach police."

The Seaside Heights Beach Patrol consists of well-trained, highly efficient lifeguards selected for ability and not for political friendship. The patrol averages about 500 rescues a year, an extremely low figure considering the throngs that splash in the surf and bay every season. Mute testimony to their efficiency lies in the fact that the resort has not had a drowning in 40 years.

Mayor Tunney never discusses the matter of beach protection now without laughingly looking back some 35 years to the time he hired the first lifeguard for the then private Freeman beach, in the struggling young resort.

"I couldn't understand why he always carried a life ring with him while on duty. I wondered about it all summer long. And then in September I made a discovery. You know something? That son-of-a-gun couldn't even swim!"

The Mayor considers the incident, on his part, was a matter of misplaced confidence rather than a lack of judgment. As for the non-swimming lifeguard, Mayor Tunney grudgingly admits the fellow deserves credit for, "courage and effort."

They are two of the characteristics in which he places great store—probably because he is so richly endowed with both himself.

He never seems to hesitate when something needs to be done. That's why his days are still filled with many activities, be they pertaining to public affairs, in connection with such organizations as the Ocean County Planning Board or the New Jersey Conference of Mayors, of which he is a director. The N. J. Resort Association and a host of others.

Somehow he manages to find time to serve in many other capacities. He is a trustee of the Community Memorial Hospital at Toms River and is the founder of the Seaside Chapter of Deborah Hospital at Browns Mills, a charitable institution open to all faiths and races without cost.

How does a man feel who has crowded so much into the years? Don't expect any flowery speeches from Joseph Stanley Tunney. He says, simply:

"It's really been something. And I've loved every minute of it."

4 ♦

The Hard Road Up

The successes of his years in public office have not made Stanley Tunney forget the trials that came before. Memories tend to become veiled in the mist of passing years, but there are many for this man that still remain in sharp focus, and he has a deep sense of pride mixed with gratitude in the fact that the road was anything but easy.

Born in Bordentown, N. J., November 26, 1885, this newcomer to the family of his housepainter father was christened Joseph Stanislaus Tunney. Early in his childhood his parents took to calling him Stanley and the name stuck.

There was elementary schooling in his home town and some training in business courses at Rider College in Trenton, but even at an early age he was well acquainted with hard work.

During World War I he worked in Philadelphia at the Frankfort Arsenal and the Midvale Steel Company. The steel company closed after the war and the young Tunney took his first crack at the real estate business.

"I soon got tired of that," he says. "It was dog eat dog with everybody trying to run over each other. I made money but I was like a caged lion. I had to get out."

He returned to Bordentown to marry Louise K. Stahle and they began their life together in Burlington operating a hardware store.

"We sold ourselves out of business," he recalls, explaining that he gave credit to contractors and others who either were too slow in making payments or didn't pay at all. And his suppliers were knocking on the door.

"The thing snowballed against me, so I turned the lock in the door. It took me 12 years to pay my bills, but I paid every penny," he says.

Meanwhile, the family had come to Seaside Heights for a vacation. That was about 1924.

"It was so nice for the family. There was so much open space. It looked like a good place for the future. There was also the fact that I didn't have enough money left to pay our carfare out."

He turned his hand to whatever work there was to be found in the young town, but he was determined to be his own boss.

Finding work as a maintenance man for Frank H. Freeman, one of the pioneer developers of the resort, he kept his eyes open for a business opportunity. The first to come was the chance to rent a Freeman-owned fishing pier.

"The chance was a good one, but I didn't have a cent to put into it. Then I learned that Mr. Freeman needed 100 pilings for a bulkhead. So I quickly went out and made a deal with a fellow, sold the piles to Mr. Freeman for a dollar profit on each one and then handed him back the $100 as down payment on the rent for the pier."

The Tunney family en masse opened a food shack on the pier as an accommodation to the fisherman who paid to use it. The business flourished but fate was unkind.

"I was washed to sea three times," he recalls. The last time was in a storm that battered the pier beyond repair.

Even with the whole family working, it was difficult to make enough money in the summer months to feed the brood of six children in winter.

"So I became a money miner," he remembers. When the summer bathers were gone he would sift the beach sands for valuables.

Every morning with a shovel and a coal sifter he would walk the beach looking for pay-dirt.

"I got to be an expert at it. I could follow a vein just like the old gold miners did. I used to average about $6 a day and I found diamonds, rings, gold and all sorts of valuables along with coins. Once I even got $15."

The Mayor said he learned from experience that money lost by vacationers on the beach during the summer eventually, through wave action worked its way to pilings. And the piles supporting the boardwalk became his favorite prospecting point.

"One day I was sort of digging around some piling when Chief McDevitt, who was then only a patrolman, came along and bawled me out—said I was undermining the boardwalk," he recalls with a laugh. "But I kept on beachcombing anyway. After all, I had six kids to feed."

"Things were pretty tough back in those days. The depression was here and—well, let's face it—like most Americans, I was broke."

Those were the days, the mayor says, when it required some of the old pioneering spirit to keep going.

"There were about 30 year-round families here then and during the winter months of the depression we lived off the beach and the bay. There was a coal shortage so we burned driftwood that we hauled away from the beach.

"When the wind blew from the west we could always pick up a mess of frost fish on the beach. And there were some fine oyster beds in the bay to vary our diet. I guess we lived pretty good at that."

Mayor Tunney remembers well the first house he built. He was located on Decatur Avenue in Seaside Park.

"No, I hadn't really left the Heights. I had a business on the boardwalk there and I claimed that as my legal residence.

"I started building with just $50. And I'll never forget the dining room. It was only eight feet wide and when you get a family of eight together around a table in a room that size there's not much open space left.

"If somebody had to leave the table during a meal they had two choices. They could duck down and crawl under the table or they could go out the front door and come in again through the back."

Of all the stories he has to tell about those early days, the

Mayor likes best the one about the incident that he believes was a turning point in his life.

Walking the lonely beach one day he spied a heavy barrel tossing about in the surf. It proved to be full of whiskey.

"It was like manna from Heaven," he says. "It was like the bank gave me a blank check to get all the money I needed. After that everything seemed to go all right."

It was on a day in the late 1920's and he had sent his wife to Burlington to draw out the last bit of money they had in the bank.

"While she was away I was walking along the beach and saw this barrel. I rolled it up to the boulevard and hailed everybody I saw in a car, trying to get help to bring it home. But nobody would stop. They must have thought there was a body in it.

"When I got it home, I took an auger and bored a hole in it. It was full of Irish whiskey and I sold it to a fellow for $300."

He caught the first train for Philadelphia and outfitted himself from top to bottom. Then he made connections with the train he knew Mrs. Tunney would be aboard on the return trip to Seaside.

"I walked up to her seat and dumped the money in her lap. There was more than $200 left."

"She looked at me and almost fainted. That money was the biggest lift we ever got. From then on things picked up for my family."

And the fortunes of the Tunney family—he now counts a total of 42 descendants when all the children, grandchildren and great-grandchildren are added up — have prospered ever since.

He and Mrs. Tunney kept their boardwalk restaurant going, meanwhile branching out into the amusement ride business. And then the arrest incident triggered his determination to enter local politics to improve the position of the beach business people.

"There are some politicians who forget that all kinds of people make up this world, and that everybody doesn't have to do or think like they do."

"You don't dictate to people what they can do and what they

can't do. You don't put a halter around their heads to stop progress.

"I never had the idea that someone in the same business would hurt me. More business brings more people here. When you get the people here and you don't do business with them, that's your fault."

5 ◆

Fire, Storm and War

The simple logic of Mayor Tunney's live-and-let-live business principles have served Seaside Heights well. And most of the obstacles placed in the path of progress have, in the last quarter century, been the work of nature and the elements.

Repeatedly through the years the people of the resort have had to fight back the storm-tossed ocean and while at times the toll of damage has been heavy it has never been insurmountable.

But nothing strikes terror into the hearts of its people like the cry of "fire!" and no one soon will forget the holocaust that swept the boardwalk early in the season of 1955.

The date of June 9 is seared in the memories of those who witnessed the destruction. It was 6 a.m., and the resort was just getting ready to greet the first seasonal influx of summer visitors.

"When they woke me I took one look out the window and I kissed it goodbye," Mayor Tunney recalls. The flames, feeding on hard pine were soaring in the air and the smoke was terrific. Fire engines were converging on the scene. Building after building and huge sections of the boardwalk were consumed. I've never seen anything like it and I never want to again, believe me."

Fanned by 50-mile an hour winds, the fire raged through three blocks of the boardwalk, devouring all in its path. It destroyed the amusement area from DuPont Avenue in the Heights to just beyond Stockton Avenue in Seaside Park in a two-hour period. The financial loss ran into millions.

But almost before the ashes had cooled men were at work to begin clearing away the debris to start the massive task of rebuilding.

Particularly heart-breaking was the loss of the old Carousel, a beachfront landmark that had stood since 1917. While the frenzied rebuilding program got underway, Mayor Tunney searched far and wide to find another merry-go-round of the same vintage.

As a boy of 13 in his native Bordentown he had carried coal to fire the steam boiler that powered a carousel there. It was a labor of love then and he never lost his feeling for them.

"I finally located one in Coney Island and bought it for $22,000. It cost another $20,000 to get it here, refit it and repaint it," he said. He personally did much of the repainting, especially the fine line work about the prancing animals that takes a steady hand and a practiced eye.

More than 50 concessions were destroyed in the blaze but before the summer season was well underway the boardwalk had been rebuilt and the scars of the fire obliterated.

The resort had waged another fight for its economic life some 10 years before.

That was during the early days of World War II when German submarines were prowling just off the New Jersey coast in wolf-packs hunting down oil tankers and supply ships that were maintaining the lifeline to American troops and their allies battling the Axis in many parts of the world.

Repeatedly during those dread times residents of the resort area saw the evidence of the enemy's work.

In the still of the night would come heavy explosions and a red glow would light up the eastern sky. Another American vessel had been torpedoed; more seamen had given their lives to the cause of freedom.

Then in the mornings, stark against the skyline would stand half-sunken hulks of burned out tankers. Survivors, burned and injured and coated with the heavy oil that had filled their ships would be brought ashore. Great deposits of oil, carried by the tides, would blacken the beaches.

It was discovered that the submarines were lying in wait within miles of the beach and that lights from the shore were silhouetting ships convoys to form easy targets for their deadly torpedoes. Something had to be done to halt them.

Then came the blackout. Street lights were dimmed or turned off completely. Lighted signs outside buildings were forbidden. Automobiles felt their way along darkened streets with the top half of their headlights painted black to reduce the glow to a minimum.

It was not a time for "business as usual" and Seaside Heights, like all towns, was sharply mindful of the duty it owed to support the nation's war effort. But it had a need to survive.

To keep some lifeblood flowing in its business veins during the summer months, and still keep faith with its fighting men, the resort struck upon a novel method to frustrate the enemy submarines off-shore.

A system of blackout curtains was designed and erected along the seaward edge of the boardwalk. They extended high enough to blot out any light that might escape from the concessions along the walk and the big advantage the subs held was snatched from them. As the toll in torpedoed tankers dropped Seaside Heights was able to function as a resort where war-weary people could find some temporary escape.

6 ◆

The Hiering Heritage

Seaside Heights has pioneered in many "firsts." One of the most valuable pieces of equipment of Seaside Heights highly-efficient public safety department is a closed circuit television monitor by which the whole town is constantly kept under surveillance. It is perhaps the only installation of its kind in the world.

An operator seated at a console can bring in a living picture of any desired spot within seconds, for the device can scan 350 degrees of the compass with only a 10-degree seaward area left uncovered. A zoom lense can be adjusted so that the camera can find a minute spot on the boardwalk or the business or residential areas. It is a highly effective tool during the summer when throngs fill the beaches and fun areas as well as during the winter when streets at night are virtually deserted.

Imagine that this TV installation is not a modern-day actuality but a device of science fiction by which time can be turned back. What would the eye of the camera reveal were the calendar to be reversed a half century?

It would see but a handful of small cottages among the dunes near the beach. Unbridged Barnegat Bay would lie to the west. Railroad tracks leading from Bay Head to the north would follow their course through the young town and on to Seaside

Park and the long wooden trestle that carried them back to the mainland.

Perhaps the camera would focus on the figure of beloved Christian Hiering strolling along gravelled and wood-curbed Sheridan Avenue. The street extended from the bay to the ocean and Mr. Hiering had it built for one prime purpose: convenience for his daily walk to the ocean.

It was a ritual he never missed. Arriving there, Mr. Hiering would search for a clam shell, fill it with sea water and drink. He was a firm believer in the health-giving qualities of the ocean; convinced that his daily drink of brine was helping the rheumatism that afflicted him when he moved to the shore from Newark in 1909.

Christian Hiering was also a firm believer in the prospects of the new community that was slowly taking form and the efforts he expended to help it grow left marks that are still visible today.

The fine home he built overlooking Barnegat Bay, now Seaside Bible Church, was one of the first three dwellings erected. He became a prime mover in the organization of the town into an incorporated borough and served on its first borough council.

Repeatedly during the 18 years he lived in Seaside Heights before his death in 1927, Mr. Hiering was offered the chance to serve as its Mayor. But he steadfastly refused, preferring to remain in the background. It was honor enough for him to give of himself and his personal wealth to help Seaside Heights flourish.

Born in Germany, Mr. Hiering came to the United States in the late 1800's. An inventor and manufacturer, he was one of the founders of the J. E. Mergott Co., in Newark.

As his interest in Seaside Heights grew, so did his business operations, including considerable real estate holdings. In 1913 Mr. Hiering founded the Barnegat Power and Cold Storage Company, which supplied both Seaside Heights and Seaside Park with their first electric power. During World War I, the company expanded its operation to enter the field of freezing fish and other foods.

One of the great needs of the young town was better access from the mainland and Mr. Hiering was one of the founders of the first toll bridge erected across Barnegat Bay in 1915.

His industrious nature was reflected in his heirs.

At an early age Albert C. Hiering began to follow in his father's footsteps. He entered the real estate and pound-fishing business and remained in those two fields until his death. He served on the Borough Council, was president of the Seaside Park Fish Company; secretary-treasurer of the power and cold storage business and secretary of the Tunney & Hiering Realty Company, of which he and Mayor Tunney were co-owners.

The Hiering name is carried on today in true family tradition by Ocean County Assemblyman William T. Hiering who also serves as Seaside Heights' borough solicitor.

The plan to develop what is now the southern half of Seaside Heights took form on January 27, 1909 when three members of the Grosscup family, Allan, Walter and George, met in Camden to organize the Manhasset Realty Company. The first order of business was to acquire for $25,000 an agreement held by Edward E. Grosscup for the purchase of the beachfront property.

The three Grosscups were the only members of the corporation at the time but a month later it was expanded to include F. C. Goodwin, J. Milton Slim, Wellington E. Barto, William Wilkie, T. F. B. Scott, Milton Close and Frank Griffenberg as directors. At the same time Mr. Goodwin became its president.

The tract had already been plotted into lots and streets and the corporation quickly began plans to sell the 855 lots. The sale of property was advertised in the Philadelphia and Camden area and handsome brochures were compiled to attract prospective land owners.

The corporation directors, however, wanted people to see the land as it really existed and hit upon the idea of conducting railroad excursions to the site. Present day land developers fly their prospects to Florida and Arizona by air. The first was held on Decoration Day, 1909, and the response was such that the excursions to Seaside Heights became a permanent practice for the next few years.

The excursionists had a chance to see how Seaside had already developed; to sample the exhilarating ocean and bay air and to dream of one day themselves living in such pleasant sur-

The first Railroad Station.

Ever ready to repel threat from fire, is a squad of local volunteers, circa 1918.

A younger edition of the man who was to become Mayor.

Built for slower traffic, the first bridges couldn't bring visitors in fast enough.

The first paid life-guard crew to man the resort's beaches. ❤

Building interest in the town via events such as parades, etc., was a popular method during its initial growth.

This group of "pirates" include residents who are s active in the community.

After the season they found that the Life Guard "couldn't swim."

Baby Parades were a novelty in the days before Boardwalk was built.

Floats created in colorful fashion, marked many of the parades staged after World War I. ▼

▲ One of the first fishing piers.

The town's residents have always been proud of their fire fighting equipment, even as far back as the early 20's.

Seaside Heights, N. J., Friday, December 5, 1924

DISABLED RUM-RUNNING BOAT BEACHED; HAS CARGO OF BRANDY AND WHISKEY

Buffeted by Waves When Engine Stops Crew Nearly lose Lives in High-rolling Sea, Driven to Shore on Tide and Boat Capsizes; Some Liquors Carried Out to Sea; Offer A. Spahner $1,000.00 to Store Liquor for One Day; Conceal Booze in Shrubbery and Bury it Underneath Boardwalk; Crowds Swarm Beach, Unearth Liquor and Carry it Away in Automobiles and Trucks

Coast Guards Seize Forty Cases of Cognac Brandy And Whiskey; Sherriff and State Troopers on Scene; Rum-Runners Return and Make Search For Lost Liquors

The people along this section of the coast were aroused from their slumbers at an early hour on Saturday morning, when a rum-running boat was beached after the crew came dangerously near losing their lives in an angry sea. So far as is known, the boat became disabled when near the beach, but was nearly driven ashore on a high tide.

That she had a large cargo of cognac brandy, Irish and Scotch whiskies was apparent by later developments. The small vessel plunged into the sandy beach and partly capsized. At the same time some of the cases of liquors were hurled overboard and some of it washed out to sea. Some of this, however, was re-whiskey. The boat that unloaded the stuff however, got away. In addition to the boat that was beached not far from Sheridan avenue, it was reported there were two other boats and that in the enchtopment use of the boats had delivered her cargo. According to reports, this was speedily taken away in high-powered trucks. It is supposed that the crew of the disabled boat were taken away on one of these fast vessels.

Sheriff Grant and some of his men were quickly on the scene, but as the affair was one for the Coast Guards to handle they made only a brief investigation. Later the Coast Guards took charge of the stranded boat, shoveled out the sand in the hold and

▲ Fire, and storm have ravaged the community. The holocaust of 1955 wiped out huge sections of the Boardwalk. They were quickly rebuilt.

As it did in every town in the U.S., Prohibition, that "noble experiment" left its mark, as indicated by this headline of almost 30 years ago from the Review, published in Seaside Heights.

One of the first bathing pavilions, popular with an earlier generation of visitors. ▼

Seaside Heights, N. J.

Upper. Gov. Richard J. Hughes, signs into law a bill sponsored by the New Jersey Amusement Board of Trade which benefits Seaside Heights and the entire amusement industry in N.J. Looking on are Mayor Tunney, president of the State organization and Mrs. Miriam Harding, a director of the State Amusement organization.

Lower ... Early day real estate developers of the boro brought in many special excursion groups from Philadelphia, Camden, Trenton and other points to sell them the charms of Seaside Heights.

roundings. In such circumstances, the task of selling property was not too difficult.

Meanwhile the Cummings Brothers, who owned the northern section of the town were also engaged in development plans.

New homes continued to spring up in the town and with them business places to cater to the new residents. The first hotels were erected, too, for those who wished to spend vacations here but lacked accommodations.

There is some conflict as to which was the first hotel in the new town. In the footnotes documenting the development, the Sheridan Inn, at Sheridan and The Boulevard, built in 1912 or 1913 by Robert F. Cummings, was called the first hotel in Seaside Heights—and, incidentally, the first place in town to sell ice cream. But elsewhere there is mention that Mr. and Mrs. Joseph Endres purchased the Sumner Hotel in 1911 to begin a proprietorship that lasted for many years.

That the town was growing was indicated in the fact that as part of Berkeley Township it represented an assessed valuation of $35,000 in 1912.

It was only natural that as leaders among the townspeople watched the community grow they began to think in terms of self-government.

The movement got underway and soon willing ears in the state legislature at Trenton were listening sympathetically.

It was a happy day when the legislature, on February 26, 1913 approved a measure to "Incorporate the Borough of Seaside Heights, in the County of Ocean," and the County Clerk called for a special election on April 22, 1913 to name the first borough officers.

Edmund C. Kramer, a native of Egg Harbor City, who had moved to Seaside Heights in 1911 to enter the building contracting and cement block manufacturing business, was chosen as the first Mayor, a position he was to fill for four consecutive two-year terms.

Elected to Borough Council were Mr. Hiering, Frederick Sayles, J. Milton Slim, Frederick Jones and Henry Clark. J. C. Tindall was the first assessor; Clyde G. Marcy, the first borough clerk and Thomas Reed, the first Justice of the Peace. Judge David Veeder was named borough solicitor at the organization meeting April 29.

Their dream, and those of all the residents had become an actuality and Seaside Heights was on its way.

Some years later, a visitor to the resort was to be moved to poetry to describe his feelings and he put into rhyme the emotions that must have motivated the founders.

The Poem was entitled simply "The Seaside Heights Coast." These are the words:

> I walked along the seashore
> and filled my hands with shells,
> I held them to my ear and heard
> a tinkling, as of bells.
> I gazed out at the ocean
> my hands upon my hips,
> and as I looked, I pondered
> on the passing of the ships.
> O'er head the sun was shining
> and the water met the sky,
> while the gulls sailed all along the beach
> from the far unto the nigh.
> The water was calm and peaceful
> as smooth as was the beach,
> stretching north and southward
> as far as eye could reach.
> I'd wondered when they told me
> how the men from Seaside boast,
> But I wondered then no longer
> when I saw the Jersey Coast.

Signed only "J. J. Trenton," the poem and the writer can be forgiven any liberties taken to contrive the rhyme, for it expressed completely the feeling that residents and visitors alike come to have for Seaside Heights.

7 ◆

The Bridge to Triumph

Nineteen Hundred and Fourteen will probably be best remembered as the year the first bridge was constructed to link Seaside Heights to the mainland. But many other things were happening too. Some of these events were of prime importance; some, by today's standards, were of little consequence, but all were part of the pattern that was taking shape.

The Ocean County Review, published by its founder, William Magill, was full of news about the town's progress—a service it still renders Seaside Heights.

Nothing was too trivial to mention!

For instance, it reported in one item that Frank Tindall had purchased a house on Dupont Avenue and that "all the single girls in town are wondering for whom Frank purchased his new home."

In the same issue would be announcements such as appeared January 2, 1914; and of paramount importance.

The advertisement said that the Seaside Heights Amusement Company had arranged for the purchase of Block 14 bounded by Sumner, Webster, Bayview and Barnegat Avenues, 200 by 475 feet, and was planning to build an amusement place fronting on Bayview Avenue containing a theater, a carousel, billiard, pool and shuffleboard rooms, several stores and a promenade pavilion on the second floor.

According to other notices in the paper you could build a summer bungalow complete for $550 and rent a four-room bungalow furnished on Hamilton Avenue for $150 per season.

The early builders, Mayor Kramer, Clyde G. Marcy, N. E. Rex, J. C. Tindall, C. Milton Stimus and R. M. Milne were kept busy building cottages and houses for year round residence as well as for summer vacationers.

The volunteer fire company that had been formed in October, 1913, was looking forward to the arrival of its new chemical equipment and the construction of a firehouse on the Sherman Avenue lots donated by Mr. Hiering.

The new apparatus cost $285 and when it arrived a special meeting was held to inspect the equipment and present badges to the members.

Clarence Anthony was chief; George Hauser, assistant chief; Pete A. Zisgen, foreman; Samuel Tollins, assistant foreman; Christian Hiering Jr., treasurer, and Joseph K. Johnson, secretary.

Before the new firehouse was constructed the fire company had to find temporary quarters for its new chemical engine, and accepted the offer of Clyde Marcy to store it in the garage under his house.

One evening, Mr. Marcy emptied his lighted pipe (some said it was a habit) in a waste basket. The paper in the basket caught fire, the fire spread to the window curtains. When firemen arrived they could not reach their new engine as the garage was directly under the burning room. They had to resort to the old bucket brigade to quench the flames.

The Peninsula Water Company operating from Artesian wells, had laid four miles of wooden water mains and borough council took steps to install fire hydrants as a protective measure.

The Barnegat Power and Cold Storage plant was under construction and two Philadelphia men, Joseph B. Vanderslice and John Rath purchased an oceanfront block and made plans to construct a Steeplechase Pier between Dupont and Porter Avenues.

Nothing caused more excitement in town, however, than the construction of the new bridge. Plans for the span were conceived by a company organized by the late Vice Chancellor

Maja Leon Berry of Toms River, and its progress was followed with great anticipation. The work suffered some delays but finally on October 23, 1914, according to The Review, "Motor cars pass over the new bridge."

It described how "Judge Berry, J. P. Evernham and friends steal a march on waiting throng. . . . Seaside Heights rejoices."

With the completion of the bridge, the route from Philadelphia to Seaside Heights was cut to about 65 miles, making Seaside the nearest resort to the Quaker City. The bridge, costing $130,000, was 24 feet wide and had a 50-foot draw span of the bascule type which was balanced by 125 tons of concrete and steel "so that one man could easily raise and lower it."

On Oct. 26th, the first team to cross the new bridge made the trip in one hour and 15 minutes. The team, owned by Clarence Anthony was driven by "Doc" Holland.

It was not until December 5th that the bridge was opened to the general public, after a staff had been selected to guard the structure, lift the draw and collect the tolls.

It cost 15 cents for one-horse carriages and wagons to cross the bridge with an additional five cents for each passenger. Seventy cents was charged for two horses and a driver; automobiles were charged 25 cents.

Loads exceeding 10 feet in width were not allowed under any circumstances and the weight limit was 30,000 pounds.

Pedestrians or bicycle riders were charged a nickel; motorcycles, 15 cents; for horses, cattle, sheep or hogs, led in droves, it was 10 cents a head. It was the same price for a wheelbarrow and one person, but one person and a hand cart, light or loaded, cost 15 cents. For children under five the bridge was free.

Although the bridge was in use, formal dedication did not come until Decoration Day, 1915, and The Review reported that the day was a "fair test for the bridge—568 automobiles crossed it." It added a footnote that the bridge "will be a money maker."

Early in the year, plans were started to construct a school and when it opened in September it was, in the words of the state building official who inspected it, "the best two-room schoolhouse in the state." Frank Tilton was hired as teacher-principal.

Plans for the Union Church were also progressing and a Post

Office had been located in the Sumner Hotel operated by Joseph Endres.

The Seaside Heights Building & Loan Ass'n. started the new year by electing as officers: Joseph J. Schritter, president; Percy H. Baker, vice president; F. J. Sayles, treasurer, William Hunter, secretary, and Charles W. Weygand, solicitor. Directors were Christian Hiering, Henry B. McLaughlin, George Ayler, Eugene Felden and James T. Milnamow. Most of these men were Philadelphians.

Early that summer Benjamin Endres opened his pool room and tobacco shop on the southwest corner of Webster Avenue and The Boulevard for business with the distinction of having the first establishment to be lighted by electricity. Charles Koch had also opened his garage and the Seaside Heights Construction Company had contracted to build a printing plant for the Shore Review Publishing Company. The plant and the weekly Shore Review, now published by Florian Beiseigel, is still doing business at the same address on The Boulevard between Blaine and Grant Avenues, and it was only through its files that the full history of Seaside Heights could be written.

The first Board of Health was organized during the summer of 1914 by Mayor Kramer and Council with Dr. George A. Jennings, Dr. Howard Dager, F. C. Goodwin, C. Milton Slim and Samuel Tollins as members.

In October, a group of business men met at the Hotel Sheridan to make plans for the organization of a town bank, which was to result in the creation of the Coast National Bank. A committee composed of Mayor Kramer, C. Heny, J. Milton Slim, J. T. Milnamow and D. T. Allard, was formed to direct the planning.

The first steps to improve the oceanfront were taken by council in November when ordinances were passed providing for grading, sidewalks and curbs on the avenues from Grant to Porter.

The year closed on a happy note as Mr. Hiering played host to the winter residents at a Christmas party at which Pete Zisgen furnished the music with a hand organ which he and contractor N. E. Rex had picked up on the beach after a Northeast blow.

8 ◆

Growing Pains

The period from 1915 to 1919 was one of great change and growth in Seaside Heights under the tenure of Mayor Edmund C. Kramer.

With a bridge now connecting the borough to the mainland, travel was much easier and borough officials were fully aware of the potential the town offered as a resort.

There were things to be done to improve borough services, such as acquiring the Peninsula Water Co., to make it a public utility; installing street lighting, obtaining a passenger and freight station for the railroad and continued improvement of the streets.

But the beachfront was the focal point of progress!

As early as 1915, officials were talking about the need of a boardwalk along the ocean and a step in that direction developed when F. C. Goodwin, president of the Manhasset Realty Company announced that the company would grant the borough riparian rights on its oceanfront property.

It was to be four years, however, before all the problems connected with such a venture could be solved. Early in 1919, council authorized a $25,000 bond issue, a contract was given to the Red Bank firm of Thompson and Matthews, Inc., and the first three blocks of the boardwalk were completed by May.

It was finished just in time for the biggest Memorial Day weekend in the young history of the resort.

The Shore Review reported on June 4th that visitors began arriving Friday night by train. On Monday when the holiday was over, so many people were waiting at the railroad station to return home that the Pennsylvania Railroad had to send a special train of 12 cars to handle the crowds. The paper boasted that the railroad ran the train directly to Seaside Heights and returned to Philadelphia as soon as it was loaded.

There were many ways in which newcomers were attracted to the growing resort, such as the invitation to a grand auction sale the Manhasset Realty Company extended in August, 1915.

To liquidate its holdings the company said it would offer 183 improved residence lots at auction until every one was sold for whatever it would bring. Bidders could get easy terms or a discount for cash.

The advertisement said "Free, $2000 in valuable souvenirs. Band concerts every day. Boxes of delicious chocolates for the ladies. Good 10-cent cigars for the men."

That same summer the Senate Amusement Company began construction of the Carousel and other amusement facilities on the beachfront between Dupont and Porter Avenues, and in a special election, the voters, backing the principle of municipal ownership, overwhelmingly approved a bond issue for $35,000 to buy the water works and $15,000 to supply electric power.

The borough's street lighting was turned on for the first time on June 30, 1916 to light the resort's way to a new era.

The Seaside Heights Yacht Club was growing, too. It had purchased a bayfront building at Dupont Avenue and was running chartered Barnegat Bay trips on the Ariella and Dorianna. In September the club staged its first regatta on the bay in which motorboats competed.

Almost as exciting as the coming of electric power for lighting of streets, was the opening on July 1, 1916 of the first motion picture theater.

The 450 seat theater was constructed by Albert C. Lewis at the corner of Stockton Avenue and The Boulevard. Admission was 10 cents for matinees and 15 cents for evening performances, and the inaugural films presented Mary Pickford in "Rags" and Charlie Chaplin in "Work." Special arrangements were made to convey patrons to and from the Colonial by jitney (bus) or horse-drawn stage for three cents each way.

Many times during the period there was talk that Seaside Heights and Seaside Park would combine into one municipality. But the plans never materialized because Heights officials and residents alike preferred to remain independent.

Mayor Kramer was serving his fourth term when he decided to resign in 1919 and precipitated the strangest political situations in Seaside Heights' history.

To fill the vacancy left by the Mayor's resignation, Council chose Dr. G. Gould Lawyer, one of its members, but he had to stand for reelection the following November.

Opposition developed to his continuation in office and Frank H. Freeman, one of the town's pioneer builders and a major property owner, entered the September primary and won the Republican nomination for Mayor in a sticker campaign.

The heated campaign generated in the primaries carried over into the general election in November and when the votes were counted Mr. Freeman was returned a victor over Dr. Lawyer by a vote of 30 to 27.

But Dr. Lawyer didn't give up without a fight. He challenged Mr. Freeman's election in court, charging that seven votes for the latter were cast by voters who were not legal residents.

Consequently, when it came time for council to reorganize on January 1, 1920, Dr. Lawyer presided at one meeting and Mr. Freeman presided at another. Each appointed his own council committees and his own borough officers.

At one stage, the firehouse in which the municipal offices were located was padlocked. When Dr. Lawyer and the councilmen who supported him arrived their entrance was barred.

The locks were quickly broken, however, because in case of fire, firemen would be unable to reach their equipment.

The dual administrations went their separate ways, setting up budgets, passing ordinances and conducting other borough business.

It was not until April 30, 1920 that Mr. Freeman was upheld in a court ruling that struck only one name off the registration list, leaving him the victor by a margin of just two votes.

The borough also passed through another crisis that same year when a move was made to abolish public dancing on Sundays. The campaign that followed was just as heated as the election campaign just passed, but the ordinance was eventually defeated.

With those controversies out of the way Council was able to get down to business once more and before the end of the year a contract was let for the completion of the north end of the boardwalk.

The Mayor's seat was to change hands several times before the arrival of Mayor J. Stanley Tunney on the political scene.

Mr. Freeman was defeated in the 1921 election by Frederick Jones. Mr. Kramer was elected Mayor again in 1923 and served another two-year term. Dr. Lawyer made a new bid for the position in the 1925 election and began what was to be a six-year tenure until his defeat in 1931 by Alfred W. Borden. Charles A. Smith was Mayor Borden's successor and served in office until his death on July 28, 1939. Edward Ryan, Sr. completed his term until the election of Mayor Tunney.

To all of these men who served as chief executives of the borough, and the many who served with them in elective and appointive positions, go a share of the credit for the continued growth of the resort community.

There were times, of course, of disagreement on the methods to be used to improve Seaside Heights as there is bound to be in any democratic society. But never was there any dispute over the ultimate aim. And generally, when the furore of the moment was over, another progressive step was under way.

Throughout the 1920's and even in the early depression years of the 1930's, Seaside Heights continued to grow.

Development of the northern section of the boardwalk began as early as March, 1920, and other improvements were made in the years ahead. Helping to clear the way were such unselfish acts as the gift to the borough made by Mayor Freeman in 1921 from his personal land holdings of a valuable 20-foot wide strip from the Carousel to the Seaside Park line.

It was a pattern to be followed by other land-owners and business firms in later years. In 1923, Joseph Endres and the Coast Amusement Company syndicate bought the F. P. Larkin tract, one block wide and extending from the beachfront to the railroad, for amusement and business development. A few years later the company deeded land for a street through the tract that helped greatly in establishing better traffic movement.

Mr. Endres also was a leader in the movement to organize the town's first bank and served as treasurer of the institution when it opened its doors as the Coast National Bank under a charter granted in April, 1923 when Seaside Heights was just 10 years old as an incorporated municipality. H. Ross Turner, the president, proudly announced that 150 persons had deposited $75,000 in the new institution at Webster and The Boulevard on the first day of business—June 4, 1923.

Another significant development for the resort came in March, 1920, when the state legislature authorized the purchase of the privately-owned bridge over Barnegat Bay. It was two years later that purchase by a state commission for $168,000 was consummated and the span became toll-free. The following winter $83,000 was spent in repairs to the bridge and then in 1926 $300,000 was authorized for rebuilding the 7100-ft bridge. The new structure was opened for use on Decoration Day, 1927, marked by a seven-mile-long parade. On Labor Day 6,940 cars passed over the span.

At the same time the borough was beginning work to bulkhead the bayfront and the county constructed a concrete road from the bridge to Toms River.

In 1927 the borough's assessed valuation passed the million mark and development continued. A sewer system was installed in 1928 and the next year a Bay boulevard was started.

All of these signs of progress notwithstanding, there was one woman visitor who apparently remained oblivious to the fact that Seaside Heights had grown up. Arrested for bathing "au naturel," she complained that she had seen no signs forbidding it. Justice of the Peace James H. Rice waved her protest aside:

"Signs or no signs," he said, "You know we are not living in the days of Adam and Eve."

The tide of progress was to take an unhappy turn as the depression spread in the early 1930s. Like all areas of the country, Seaside Heights felt the pinch. A heavy blow came when the bank, whose control had passed to outside interests, was closed and placed in receivership, never to reopen.

Planning for capital improvements had to be dropped and the borough council began a retrenchment program. Salaries of borough employees were reduced and other steps to meet the financial crisis were taken. Some refinancing of borough indebtedness was necessary but the borough never defaulted on its state and county taxes.

Tested in adversity, the town bravely weathered the years of hardship and was among the communities which early found a way out of the depression and into a new era of prosperity.

God has spared some of the early pioneers to witness the fruition of their plans and dreams that began a half century ago. But time has taken its toll.

The community was saddened last Aug. 26, by the death of former Mayor Kramer at 85, just a few months short of the golden anniversary date. Although his career as a public official had long since ended, he remained an ardent and loyal worker for the betterment of Seaside Heights. His wife, Mrs. Mary Esher Kramer, once herself a member of the borough's official family, whom he married in June, 1925, is still living in the town.

In tribute to the first mayor's memory, Mayor Tunney and the Borough Council decreed that the name of the Boulevard will be changed for the duration of the anniversary year to Edmund C. Kramer Boulevard.

9 ♦

A World of Fun

Seaside Heights challenges the world to produce an equal to its great boardwalk amusement center. With nearly 500 rides, concessions and attractions, the resort's officials claim that its concentration of amusements outstrips any other facility of its kind in the universe. They do not hesitate to include Disneyland, in California; Freedomland in New York; Palisades Park in New Jersey, the famed Tivoli in Copenhagen or Brighton in England when issuing such a challenge.

Supporting this proud claim is the colorful spectacle the beachfront presents when the vacation season is in full bloom. The hum of gyrating rides, the babble of happy thousands at play, the cries of concessionaires intermingle against a rainbow-hued background to present a panorama of gaity and fun. At night, countless lights in myriad patterns set the velvety darkness of summer skies aglow, sending out a message that here is pleasure unlimited.

Seaside Heights is a town of people having fun!

The genesis of this merriment can be traced back virtually to the beginning of the borough itself, and to the foresight of one man. By today's standards, it was a humble start that the late Frank H. Freeman made in 1916 when he took over an enterprise that had already been marked for failure.

In 1915 Joseph B. Vanderslice of Philadelphia, had built a

pavilion on the beach between Porter and Dupont Avenues and installed a gasoline-powered merry-go-round. But the venture failed in its first season.

Mr. Freeman, who was later to serve a term as Seaside Heights' Mayor, took over the following summer and breathed new life into it. The old merry-go-round was replaced by a fine, new carousel, this one turned by electricity. Other attractions were added to gain and hold the interest of vacationists. Year by year the Freeman Amusement Center grew, until today it contains more than 50 concessions—including, of course, a carousel.

Ownership is still retained, to a large degree, by Freeman descendants. It is operated by the Belle Freeman Estate, in which a daughter, Mrs. Greta Freeman Rundle of Pittsburgh and Seaside Heights, and her three daughters, have a substantial interest.

The Freeman establishment holds a prime place along with two other major centers that dominate the boardwalk amusement scene. One is the Casino, operated at the north end by the Venice Amusement Corporation; the other is Funtown, U.S.A., located at the south end of Seaside Heights and extending into Seaside Park, operated generally under the aegis of the Seaside Operating Co., Inc.

The Casino amusement complex covers a beachfront block from Grant to Sherman Avenues and extends from the ocean, with riparian rights, to the Boulevard. It includes a 500 foot pier extending over the ocean. There is a 165 x 65 foot Olympic swimming pool, the largest recirculating salt water pool in the country and a ballroom that is a center for teenage dancers nighly during the summer. The main Casino building contains a carousel and other rides, concessions and an arcade. There are 35 rides, plus 50 games and other concession stands on the pier.

Operation of the Casino is under the direction of Kenneth Wynne, Jr., son-in-law of John FitzGerald, Jr., of New Haven, Conn., the principal owner.

The Venice Amusement Corporation, is the parent company of the Atlantic Land Corp., the Heights Corp., the Coast Corp., and the Ocean Corp.

The Venice group took over operation of the center 15 years

ago when it acquired the property from Linus Gilbert, Princeton contractor, who was the original developer. Members of the corporation then were Mr. FitzGerald and John Christopher and David Simon, both of New York City. A year later Mr. Simon sold his interest to the other partners, who began development of the center to what it is today.

Mr. Christopher died in 1959 and in January 1960 Mr. FitzGerald purchased the interests of the Christopher Estate to become sole owner. He commissioned Mr. Wynne to take over active management of the Venice operations. At the present time a new corporation is being organized consisting of the elder FitzGerald, his son, J. B. FitzGerald and Mr. Wynne.

Mr. Wynne took leave from his television film producing firm in Connecticut to devote full time to his new duties with Venice, and has remained in that capacity since. A resident of North Haven, Conn., he is a graduate of Trinity College, Hartford, and the Law School of the University of Connecticut. He served as administrative assistant to Chester Bowles when the latter was governor of Connecticut and has directed many political campaigns for other Connecticut figures, including U.S. Senator Abraham Ribicoff.

Mr. Wynne's television production company specializes in educational and children's films, but it also produced in color a film titled "Sun and Fun in Seaside Heights," which has become an important promotional vehicle for the Borough's amusement facilities.

Mr. Wynne is also a founder-director of the New Jersey Amusement Owners' Board of Trade, and an active participant in its activities.

Funtown U. S. A., emerged out of the ruins of the disastrous boardwalk fire of 1955. Its amusement facilities cover four full beachfront blocks on property of Belle Freeman Estate and Rundle & Tunney along the Boardwalk from Dupont Avenue in Seaside Heights to Stockton Avenue in Seaside Park and extend over a two block area from the boardwalk to Ocean Terrace.

The combined efforts of a group of individuals and business firms were thrown into the construction which began in 1956 to be ready for opening to the public in the spring of 1957.

There are 18 major rides and 15 kiddie rides. The Sky Ride,

a monorail type, was the first of its kind in this country when it was completed in 1961. Another first, claimed by Funtown is the Sun Valley Bob. An import from Germany, it is a product of Funtown management's practice of sending representatives annually to Europe in search of new ideas. The newest kiddie ride, installed a year ago, is a miniature turnpike, realistic in every detail.

Besides the rides the Funtown complex includes 121 concessionaires operating such attractions as gift shops, shooting galleries, skill games and arcades.

Seaside Operating Company is a corporation with 11 directors representing other companies operating within the amusement center.

William P. (Pat) Tunney, son of Mayor J. Stanley Tunney, is president; Max M. Warner, head of Seaview Amusement Company, is vice president; Miriam C. Harding, secretary, and Richard Chabok, treasurer. Other directors include Mayor Tunney, Edward F. Groffie, who is Mr. Tunney's son-in-law, Anthony Ricci, Carl Mahlstedt, Louis Dello Russo, Robert Lysak and William Novograd.

Among the companies they represent are Rundle & Tunney Corp., Belle Freeman Estates, Tunney & Groffie Company, and Carousel Arcade, Inc.

The major rides in Funtown are operated by Seaview Amusement Company, and the kiddie rides by Tunney & Groffie.

The group recently added to its holdings by the acquisition of an adjoining building on Ocean Terrace which is called the Funtown Reception Center. Covering a full block, the center contains such facilities as bath houses, luncheonette, soda fountain, ballroom and a charter bus receiving area.

Contemplated for the early future is an Olympic-size swimming pool and motel facilities, part of a plan to make it available as a convention headquarters. Construction of a pier over the ocean as an extension of the main Funtown area is also in the planning stage.

Between the two amusement giants at either end of the boardwalk are hundreds of other concessions, smaller but no less important links in the chain that makes Seaside Heights a great playland.

Shown with an oil portrait of her husband presented him by friends and admirers after getting the Boardwalk back into operation quickly after the devastating fire of 1955, is the late Mrs. Louise K. Tunney, whose activities in the boro were numerous during her lifetime.

Freeholder A. Paul King, a veteran leader of Ocean County, receives from the Mayor the newly adopted official flag of Seaside Heights, a feature of its Golden Anniversary celebration.

Part of the modern equipment and the staff of the municipal maintenance department which make the town a modern place in which to live and visit.

Boro officials include (left to right) Tax Collector, August Speier; Senior Clerk, Miss Barbara Foley; Boro Clerk, James Fraser; Mrs. Edith Dirkin and William Rooney. ▼

Through TDI (Transportation Displays, Inc., N.Y.) millions of motorists are made aware of the lure of Seaside Heights via colorfully painted signs on railroad bridges throughout the state.

Main business street of the Boro with its wide variety of year round and seasonal stores.

◀ The broad, safe beaches are among the most popular along the entire stretch of famous Jersey Coast.

10 ◆

Safety on the Beaches

The safety of the countless thousands of visitors who bathe in its invigorating ocean and bay waters is of paramount importance to Seaside Heights. And to maintain a record unblemished by a drowning in 36 years, the resort has developed a beach patrol system that has revolutionized life-saving practices into a fine art.

Two "firsts" have been incorporated into the program. Seaside Heights is the first community to use closed-circuit television and the first to employ an off-shore patrol boat to augment a force of 35 skilled lifeguards.

The unified system, first put into operation a year ago, has become a model that has attracted the attention of other resorts everywhere. Repeatedly during the summer of 1962 Capt. John Boyd, director of the Beach Patrol, played host to official visitors from other communities and demonstrated the efficiency of the system. Without exception, they acknowledged it to be the finest ever devised for maintaining the security of beach and surf.

The investment in the television and boat equipment has been returned a hundred-fold in the life-saving missions they have helped the patrol to accomplish and maintain the borough's spotless record of safety.

That is a record that Capt. Boyd has guarded jealously for

the 33 years that he has headed the Beach Patrol. His dedication to the task is shared by two brothers who serve under him. Lieut. Joseph Boyd is skipper of the Miss Seaside Heights, the speedy 28-foot, twin-engined patrol boat and Lieut. Hugh Boyd is in charge of the 35-man lifeguard detachment.

It is another example of family tradition that has helped Seaside Heights grow to such eminence as a resort. Another brother, James, serves as borough engineer. They are the sons of the late Borough Councilman, Hugh J. Boyd.

Life-saving is more of a "vacation" than "vocation" with the three Boyd brothers who maintain the beach watch. When summer is over Capt. John returns to his position as football coach of Atlantic City High School; Lieut. Hugh Boyd takes up his duties as principal of Seaside Heights Elementary School and Lieut. Joseph Boyd turns again to the role of football coach and athletic director of Central Regional High School.

The closed-circuit television monitor helps the beach guardians see where the eye can't reach. It permits the officers to watch bathers anywhere on the oceanfront from Beach Patrol headquarters located at Sumner Avenue and the boardwalk.

The TV camera is mounted on a tower and can be dialed to sweep the entire expanse of surf, beach and boardwalk. A zoom lense permits the duty officer to focus on the tiniest object.

Should he see someone in trouble at sea, or someone violating beach rules, such as playing ball, or someone pilfering a purse or wallet from a beach blanket, he can call for help to handle the situation over a loudspeaker system or by telephone to the nearest lifeguard stand. The telephone system, which links each stand with patrol headquarters, was initiated in 1948, the first of its kind in New Jersey.

The television system has also proved its worth as a finder of lost children. Sometimes a child will be spotted by the monitor wandering aimlessly in tears along the beach, almost a certain sign that he is lost. Even before the child is reported lost, an announcement goes out over the loudspeaker. The child's description and location on the beach is broadcast, and soon the youngster is back with his family.

When parents report a lost child, they are given a seat before the monitor and the TV camera scans the beach until they spot their young one. Then the family is quickly reunited.

When the beaches close for the day, the television system is again taken over by the Police Department under Chief Joseph P. McDevitt. There is a second set in police headquarters, and the two are used to maintain order among boardwalk crowds and to handle traffic problems. During the off-season police find the system a helpful ally in maintaining a fire watch over the borough.

Teamed up with the television system, the patrol boat has become a valuable partner in water safety. The handsome and speedy sea skiff is equipped with ship-to-shore radio, a police radio, resuscitation equipment and other safety accessories. It has a flying bridge and twin 215 horse power engines.

The Miss Seaside Heights is docked at Pelican Island and comes out of Barnegat Inlet to patrol the beaches daily.

Its value is probably best described by the report compiled by its skipper after its first year of service.

During the 1962 season the Miss Seaside Heights effected the rescue of 19 bathers in trouble on its own, and assisted lifeguards on the beach in numerous other instances. These rescues covered the entire bathing area from Hiering Avenue on the northern borough extreme to Dupont Avenue at the south end.

As a change of pace, Lieut. Joseph Boyd, the skipper, and his mate, lifeguard Dion Feltrie, also gave the police department an assist in one instance. The boat crew spotted two men behaving in a suspicious manner under the pier. They quickly relayed the information by radio to lifeguards on the beach, who in turn called police. The pair was soon in custody.

Beyond routine patrol work, the "PT-1" as the Miss Seaside Heights is known on police radio airways, sped to help in a submersion case north of neighboring Chadwick. It reached the scene in seven minutes where a trip by car would have taken the mission 30 minutes due to heavy traffic conditions.

The Miss Seaside Heights towed six disabled power and sail boats to safety and helped many ocean and bay boatmen who were experiencing minor difficulties.

The report concluded that "All in all, the Patrol Boat experiment has been a highly successful venture. This craft has not only carried out its assigned duties successfully but it has also given our bathers an unparalleled feeling of confidence and well-being as they cavort on our beaches."

The patrol boat was called on many times by the Coast Guard to assist in answering requests for help. It also cooperated with the helicopter patrol service maintained by the New Jersey Department of Conservation.

By land, by sea and by air, the finest protection possible is offered, so that visitors to Seaside Heights can swim with confidence and in safety.

11 ✦

Protection and Service

Present-day Seaside Heights modern in every respect, is well-equipped for its role as a great resort. A fine modern brick building at Sherman Avenue and the Boulevard houses a complex of municipal departments from which all public facilities and services are directed.

Law enforcement has been under the direction of Police Chief Joseph P. McDevitt since the police department was formally organized under Civil Service in 1944. The department is staffed by 12 men the year around with the force expanded to 30 for the busy summer season. Besides regular police duties the department also handles parking meter and traffic regulation operations.

The police are well-equipped with patrol cars linked by three-way radio contact and other devices necessary to handle the problems that necessarily arise in dealing with such large and volatile summer population.

Of all its fine equipment, the department takes most pride in the closed-circuit television monitoring system. Other municipalities use television but the Seaside Heights installation is unique in that it provides virtually complete scanning of the entire community from a fixed point.

From monitors installed at two points, one at municipal headquarters and the other at lifeguard headquarters on the boardwalk, it is possible for a single officer sitting at a console in head-quarters to maintain visual contact with any location in town.

This type of surveillance permits a highly efficient coverage using a minimum of manpower. The installation has proven its worth over and over again in maintaining police contact with huge boardwalk and beach crowds and heavy traffic concentrations in summer. In the winter it serves a highly useful purpose of maintaining a fire-watch over the borough when many of the homes are unoccupied and street traffic is at a minimum.

In the early days of the resort law enforcement officers had the title of marshalls. First to hold that position was Peter A. Zisgen, who was appointed by the first borough council in 1913. He remained a resident of Seaside Heights until his death in January of 1961. In those early days the town marshall worked a 12-hour day for a salary of $2.25. Another who served the borough in earlier days as a law-enforcement officer was Frank B. Droughman, who died in March, 1961.

Chief McDevitt began his police career in 1935 when he was appointed Marshall. Four years later he was appointed chief by Mayor Tunney. At the same time he assumed other duties with the official family. At one time he was tax collector. And over the years he has served as Borough Treasurer, president of the Triboro first aid squad, president of the fire company, welfare director, chairman of the local assistance board, member of the sinking fund commission and public relations director.

When the department was formally established by ordinance in 1944, Edward J. Ryan was named lieutenant and John J. Bellange was named sergeant to serve under Chief McDevitt. The present lieutenant is Edward Groffie who also holds the position of assistant public relations director.

The Fire Department, like the police department, is well-equipped for its part in maintaining public safety. Since the early days of the volunteer organization, which is as old as the borough itself, it has grown from a small group of public-spirited men who fought fires with a hand-drawn chemical wagon, and before that a bucket brigade—to a finely-trained outfit that boasts of the best of equipment.

Housed in the borough building are a 75-foot Peter Persh aluminum aerial truck; a 750-gallon Ward-LaFrance pumper;

a 750-gallon Ford pumper; a 500-gallon Cosmopolitan pumper; an emergency truck which also has a 200-gallon pump and a rescue truck equipped with oxygen and other life and property saving devices.

Directing the activities of the department is Dell Hopson who has served as its chief for 20 years. He has become a prominent fire-fighting figure not only in his home borough but throughout New Jersey. Chief Hopson is president of the Ocean County Fire Chief's Association; president of the New Jersey State Fire College and a member of the regional board of directors of the International Fire Chief's Association.

The borough department lost its last charter member with the death of Mr. Zisgen but the exempt list is filled with the names of the men who have given dedicated service throughout the 50-year history of the town.

Other key facilities of the borough are the water, electrical distribution, and sewer systems. Leonard J. Ipri is now serving as coordinator of public works, preparatory to the retirement of Vernon C. Casler, rounding out a long tenure as Borough Superintendent. Luther Edwards is director of the water commission which operates the water service supplied by the borough of Pelican Island and Ortley Beach.

The borough is also served by the Tri-Boro First Aid Squad which covers an area including Seaside Heights, Seaside Park and Lavallette. It was incorporated in 1938 through the efforts of a committee that included Mayor Tunney, Carl Haag, the late Andrew Wickhan and the late Frederick Reeger. Prior to that time the borough had depended on the Point Pleasant Squad for assistance in first aid emergencies.

Seaside Heights children receive their early education in a well run public school covering grades one through six. The school, located at Sherman and Sheridan Avenues near Ocean Terrace, has an enrollment of 100 pupils. The principal since 1952, Hugh Boyd, succeeded Paul Hershey who had filled the position since 1922. The borough sends 100 secondary education students to Central Regional High School in Berkeley Township. Others attend Parochial School.

Banking facilities are provided by the Seaside Heights Branch of the First National Bank of Toms River. Frank W. Sutton, Jr., is president of the Bank, which was opened in 1944 after the town had been without a bank for 10 years following the closing of the Coast National Bank during the depression.

An important force in community life is Shore Boro Post No. 351, American Legion, which was organized in 1946 and granted a charter in 1948. Police Chief McDevitt was the first commander and the present leader is Armando Cocci. The post erected its present home at Carteret Avenue and Bay Boulevard in 1952. As a part of the golden anniversary celebration the post will establish a permanent memorial to Seaside Heights veterans of all wars in front of the Legion home.

Borough business people have one service club, the Rotary Club of Seaside which was organized in 1948 to cover Seaside Heights, Seaside Park and Lavallette. Samuel Wiener, pioneer department store operator, was first president and William Wittenberg heads the club now.

It would be impossible to document the contributions that have been made to the growth and development of Seaside Heights over the years by all the families that have called it "home."

There have been many which put their roots down in the early years and have continued to grow and flourish as the community progressed. In tribute to all those—named and unnamed in these pages—we trace the history of a typical Seaside Heights family: the McDevitts.

Patrick McDevitt, and his wife, Mary, first came to Seaside Heights in the summer of 1918 from Philadelphia. A year later they established a business in a two-story building erected for them by builder Clyde G. Marcy at 308 Boulevard. There were eight children in the McDevitt family.

Originally the business consisted of a grocery and clam bar, but the elder McDevitt soon found himself engaged in something entirely different. He began to get requests from people who were building homes in the new town to obtain hardware and paints for them. Shortly, he found that he was dealing more in hardware and materials than in groceries and eventually the former line supplanted the latter.

The McDevitts were in the hardware business to stay. Patrick, who served on Borough Council for nine years, from 1927 to 1936, and his wife are both deceased, but their children have kept the name alive and exceedingly active.

The alert Police Department under Chief Joseph P. McDevitt and Lieutenant Edward F. Groffie include (L to R) Patrolmen Fred Rose, John Byrne, William Sommeling, Sgt. Harry Smith, Chief McDevitt, Lt. Groffie, Sgt. William Polhemus, Patrolman Henry Lee, Dispatchers Walter Tepper, George Bassinder, James Manning.

The present active roster of the Seaside Heights Volunteer Fire Department includes the following members, listed alphabetically: William Bunting, John Byrne, Henry Cain, William Casler, Ray Chaney, Robert Cummings, Andrew Gabriel, Ward Gabriel, Henry Gilmore, Edward Groffie, Gerald Graichen, Paul K. Hershey, Kenneth Hershey, Chief Dell Hopson, Warren Hopson, William Hopson, Robert Iasillo, Leonard Ipri, Charles Kessler, William Knapp, Sanford Lawyer, President Irvin Lees, John Lutz, Guido Mazzanti, Jr., Hugh McDevitt, Joseph McDevitt, William Polhemus, Anthony Raymond, Thomas Reutter, Martin Scharf, Harry Smith, James Snively, John Snow, Ralph Speier, Patrick Tunney, William Waller, Fred Rose, Russel Koch.

The Famous Seaside Heights Beach Patrol—(kneeling left to right): Dion Feltri, Anthony Raniero, Sonny B., James O'Donnell, Lt. Hugh J. Boyd, (standing): Fred Berg, James Reed, Frank Salzer, Donald Abramowitz, (standing left to right): Lt. Joe Boyd, Russell Bension, Bob Omert, Albert Reicherz, Albert Frazer, Harry Lafko, Tom Condon, Barry Lardiere, Dave Copson, Bob Ellis, Marty Dryer, Herm Wacker, Wayne Tomalo, Joe Raniero, Capt. John J. Boyd.

PRE-PRIMARY, FIRST & SECOND — (Reading Left to Right, Bottom Row): Frances Pirone, Bridget Mc Grath, Michael Griggs, William Youmans, Billie Jo Pusey, Joy Potoka, Janet Mc Kelvey, Barbara Snow, Virginia Carrington, Diana Tocci, Brent Speier, William Casler, Gary Swayze, and Donna Guerino. (Middle Row): Mrs. Viola Verdier, Joanne Hatrak, Cathy Boyd, Peter Nemeth, Raymond Andreovla, Gary Cameron, Michael Caruso, William Sommeling, Jamie Gabriel, Thomas Carrington, Francis Werner, Donna Lundquist, Terresita Lopez, Carol Lundquist, Elizabeth Christie, Terry Eichert, Yvonne Capral, and Miss Shadinger. (Top Row): Michele Rolle, Wendy Casler, John Mc Kelvey, Mark Beale, Robert Hall, Neil Mc Devitt, James Potoka, Kevin Smith, Kim Loperfido, Debra Stock, Kathleen Casey, and Pamela Boyd.

THIRD, FOURTH, FIFTH & SIXTH—(Reading Left to Right, Bottom Row): Mrs. Wilkinson, David Smith, Michael Hatrak, Joseph Caruso, and Jeffrey Walters. (Second Row). Catherine Mc Call, Roxann Carrington, Michele Peterson, Michael Horant, Kevin Casey, Michael Casey, Leslie Yaeger, James Stock, James Griggs, Douglas Hamer, Michael Boyd, John Twist, James Chaney, Mr. Hugh J. Boyd Jr., Principal. (Third Row): Mr. Phillip Armstrong, John Beale, Andrea Walters, Judy Casler, Doreen Chabok, Lorraine Polhemus, Jacqueline Stock, Carol Chaney, Susan Byrne, James Potoka, Christopher Mesanko, Michael Werner, Jon Potoka, John Hatrak, John Di Rienzo, John Byrne. (Top Row): Fred Hamer, Robert Verdier, John Karcich, Daniel Mc Grail, Craig Borton, Donna Carrington, Martha Verdier, Suzanne Ipri, Shelley Golden, Holly Yaeger, Barbara Youmans, Debra Lundquist, Judy Stock, Jacqueline Boyd, Linda Casler.

CENTRAL REGIONAL—BOYS (Reading Left to Right, Bottom Row): Phillip Siebell, William Mc Grath, Robert Smith, Peter Stock, William Werner, Robert Slevin, Earl Swayze, Gregory Mesanko, Joseph Boyd, Larne Gabriel, Kenneth Behring, Alan Lawyer, Robert Heffernan. (Middle Row): Richard Reutter, John Wiley, Gene Potoka, Donald Hopson, Joseph Kostiha, William Culmone, David Bassinder, Patrick Tunney, Martin Scharf, Wayne Lee, Jack Snow, Dennis Poane, Steven Vandergrift, Buddy Tocci, Nelson Lopez, William Meredith, Armando Cocci, Glen Swayze, Christopher Brown. (Top Row): Timmy Cavanaugh, William Kessler, Richard Norcross, James Davis, Lenard Walencikowski, Kirk Suhoskey, Craig Sodl, John Masters, Harry Bassinder, Gerard Frunzi, Robert Kahn, George Mc Devitt, Robert Iasillo, William Chaney, Victor Simari, Anthony Di Guilio, Albert Nemeth.

ST. JOSEPH PAROCHIAL SCHOOL—(Reading Left to Right, Bottom Row): Shawn McDevitt, Kathleen McDevitt, Rita Dishon, Gay Mazzanti, Kathy Willis, Patricia Mc-Devitt, Randy Tunney, James Dishon, William Newnam. (Top Row): Vincent Procassini, Gail Mazzanti, Patricia Rolle, Linda McDevitt, Karen Beale, Joseph Tunney, Guy Mazzanti, Gerald Newnam.

CENTRAL REGIONAL—GIRLS (Reading Left to Right, Bottom Row): Margaret Newnam, Susan Groffie, Elaine Scott, Gloria Gabriel, Joan Bentz, Mary Jo Di Rienzo, Frances Snow, Barbara Sommers, Barbara Carrington, Marlene Sodl, Bren Karcich, Joni Walters, Elaine Walker, Ann Furr. (Top Row): Patricia Martucci, Sandra Bunting, Jean Ipri, Louise Kostiha, Judy Beth Brown, Joyce Raymond, Sandra Nichols, Nancy Loperfido, Carol Menschner, Ruth De Shay, Dolores Nichols, Lee Tocci, Pamela Sodl, Ann Cole, Mary Margaret Reutter.

"The history of the 'next fifty' years rests with this generation of our school children."

Our Lady of Perpetual Help, R.C. Church, Father Thomas Barry, pastor. ➤

Union Church. Rev. Robert Hall, pastor.

Seaside Bible Church. Rev. Eugene Patoka, pastor.

Three sons, all younger brothers of Police Chief Joseph P. McDevitt, now carry on the family business at the same Boulevard address. They are Hugh, James and John.

Hugh has been a councilman for nine years and is past commander of the American Legion Post; past president of the Rotary Club; a former vice-president of the Fire Company and a former captain of the First Aid Squad. James is a former assistant Postmaster and former president, captain, treasurer and secretary of the First Aid Squad; John is a Major in the Air Force Reserve.

Three of the four McDevitt daughters are still living. Elizabeth, now Mrs. Frank Miller, is a teller for the Jersey Shores Savings & Loan Association. She is a former member of the Seaside Park Board of Education and the Central Regional High School Board of Education, of which her husband is now president. Margaret, now Mrs. Charles Miller—the sisters married brothers—is a member of the election board in Seaside Park and organist and an active worker in St. Catherine's Parish. She is employed by the New Jersey Natural Gas Company and her husband is superintendent of public works in Seaside Park. Irene, and her husband, Robert Wickham, operate a restaurant supply business in the Seaside area.

It is this type of active family participation that has helped Seaside grow to greatness.

12 ✦

Tribute to God

Religion has always played an important role in the community life of Seaside Heights. The desire of its early settlers for spiritual guidance manifested itself at the very inception, growing in force as the town moved ahead. The evidence of this growth is visible today in the three fine churches which grace the resort. They are the Union Church, Our Lady of Perpetual Help R.C. Church and Seaside Bible Church of the Evangelical Presbyterian Synod. Union Church dates back to the first year of Seaside Heights' incorporation; the other two were founded in 1942.

Early records of the Union Church relate that the Founders met on August 17, 1913 to organize the Seaside Heights Sunday School, and elected J. C. Tindall as superintendent. Even with the handicap of not having a church building, interest in the program was enthusiastic. Early meetings were held at the home of Mayor and Mrs. Kramer on Hamilton Avenue (now Seaview Avenue) and at the Coast Guard Station.

It was later in that same summer that the Manhasset Realty Company donated two lots on Franklin Avenue to be used exclusively for a Union Church. The gift inspired the people to work feverishly during the following winter to realize their goal of a permanent home.

One of the great forces behind the church was a Ladies Aid

Society organized in October, 1913, with Mrs. R. Walton as president; Miss Lily Kramer, vice president; Mrs. Edmund C. Kramer, secretary and Mrs. John Barnes, treasurer.

The society conducted oyster suppers, socials and other community events as fund raising for the new church progressed and soon planning began for actual construction.

When the work began in the spring of 1914, every carpenter in the young town volunteered to give a day's work free. Christian Hiering, Sr., loaned a team of horses and a driver to cart brick for the foundation.

The cornerstone of the church was laid on Decoration Day, 1914 by John Weaver, a former mayor of Philadelphia, and the dedication services were held in August. Thus within a year, the hopes of the founders were realized.

The Rev. W. C. Boyer and the Rev. A. C. Bruckman were early pastors and Jackson Shibla, one of the early superintendents of the Sunday School is credited with being the organizer of the church choir.

The church quickly became a center of the borough's social as well as spiritual life.

The church suffered a disastrous blow on June 11, 1920 when a tornado-like windstorm demolished the structure. There was little left but the foundation when the gale had subsided and church members were numbed as they viewed the ruins.

But their faith sustained them. Immediate plans were made to rebuild and church organizations began a round of events to raise the funds. The campaign began in August with a Baby Parade and a watermelon party.

For the remainder of the summer the congregation used the Yacht Club as a meeting place. But the building lacked heat and during the fall and winter members volunteered the use of their homes for worship.

The contract to rebuild the church was finally let in February, 1921. The new building costing $4200 was completed early in the summer and the Rev. Arthur Brochman of Brooklyn presided at the dedication services on July 3. On July 22, the first baptismal in the new building took place. The child was Helen Spittal, daughter of Mr. and Mrs. William Spittal. The Rev. Rowland Nichols of Toms River, officiated.

The Rev. Robert Hall took over the pastorate of the church

in 1962 succeeding the Rev. Badon Brown who had served as minister for four years.

Although Our Lady of Perpetual Help parish is only 20 years old, Catholics among the early residents of Seaside Heights never lacked spiritual leadership.

Neighboring Seaside Park had been incorporated even before the turn of the century and the files of the Ocean County Review tell how a Catholic Priest, the Rev. Gregory Schenermann, O.M.C., came to celebrate Mass for a group of approximately 20 Catholics on July 16, 1905.

Father Schenermann, a professor of mathematics at the now extinct St. Francis College in Trenton, conducted the service in a cottage at 34 Fourth Avenue in Seaside Park. The cottage was owned by Scott Spence, but tenanted for the season by Mr. and Mrs. Thomas Russell and family of New York City.

That was the beginning of what was to become St. Catherine's parish.

At that time Seaside Heights was still but a barren tract owned by the Manhasset Realty Co. There was no road between Bay Head and Seaside Park, a trail among the sand dunes offering the only semblance of one. Pedestrians used the railroad tracks as a thoroughfare, carrying lanterns at night to light their way.

The Rev. William J. Brennan founded Our Lady of Perpetual Help Parish during the summer of 1942 and served as its pastor until his death on January 28, 1951. His demise saddened a parish that was already weighted by worry, for the church building had been destroyed by fire late in 1949.

Three months after the loss of Father Brennan, the Rev. Thomas Thaddeus Barry was appointed pastor of the parish and has served it since.

His canonical installation as pastor on April 22, 1951, brought new hope and vigor to the parish. Before summer began Father Barry announced that a contract for construction of a new church had been awarded. While work progressed on the structure, Father Barry each Sunday celebrated 12 Masses as visitors crowded into the Catholic Youth Organization Hall and the Casino Skating Rink.

The new church, costing $350,000 and seating 600, was dedicated on July 6, 1952 by Bishop Ahr and the parish began a decade of renewed growth under the leadership of Father Barry. Fire dealt the parish another blow in 1954 when the CYO Hall was destroyed but the loss seemed to inspire Father Barry and his parishioners to greater efforts in behalf of the Church.

A small group of Seaside Heights residents led by the Rev. Lester Bachman organized the Seaside Bible Church in May of 1942. Meetings were first held in various homes, then in the borough fire hall. Finally the present building was bought and remodeled into a church and regular services were begun.

A few months after organization, the church was received into the Bible Presbyterian (now called the Evangelical Presbyterian) denomination and the following year it was incorporated.

The first pastor of the church, Rev. Bachman, is now a minister of the Orthodox Presbyterian Church near Lancaster, Pa. He was succeeded at Seaside by the Rev. Evans Harden, who served the church for several years before resigning to go to Brazil as a missionary. The next pastor came while a student at Faith Theological Seminary to serve part time. He was John Hoogstrate, who served for two years as student-pastor before being called to a church in North Dakota.

The present pastor, the Rev. Eugene Potoka, is now in his 12th year as spiritual leader of the church, and guide of its full program of year-round activities.

13 ◆

The Red-Haired Pirate

It is not quite true that only the seagulls and other forms of wildlife inhabited the beach dunes before the arrival of the first settlers of Seaside Heights.

Long years before, the Barnegat Peninsula, like other areas of the then desolate New Jersey coast had borne the footprints of a breed of hard and hearty men who fed and prospered on the ill-fated sailing ships that fell within their greedy grasp.

This section of the coast is within the area that earned the unhappy title of Graveyard of Ships as fierce ocean-born storms took their tragic toll in ever increasing numbers. Many early day vessels, their sails shredded by howling winds, and even some of those of modern power have foundered on our shores.

But the elements were not their only enemies. Even worse were the men like those who bore such names as Kidd and Morgan and made pirating an evil but gainful profession. This stretch of coastline offered a perfect lair for those who made a bloody career of preying upon trading vessels.

But the very nature of their ghoulish business worked against them, too. Barred from any safe harbor for fear of reprisals, pirate craft were forced to spend long periods at sea, when supplies ran short. Their only recourse was to put into the numerous inlets, like Cranbury Inlet that once split the peninsula just north of town, seeking quiet waters in which to anchor while crews foraged for fresh water and food.

And many times too, legend says, they used the beaches as depositories for their ill-gotten gains.

Their footprints in the sand have long since been washed away by tides, but repeatedly through the years evidence of their presence has come to light.

Treasure hunting has always held a deep fascination for those who walk the beaches and ponder the mysteries of the sea. Periodically, coins and other articles are found that are believed to be tell-tale clues to buccaneering. Great discoveries of buried treasure still elude the most persistent seekers, but one of the most positive—and grisly—signs of pirateering along the coast was discovered right here in Seaside Heights.

It was the finding of the red-haired skeleton, the bones of which still rest here.

The story is best told by Vernon G. Casler, long-time borough superintendent, one of Seaside's first residents.

"In the summer of 1909, my mother and I moved from Newark to take up residence with the Stimus family, one of the three families who had homes in what was to be the Borough of Seaside Heights. The other families were the Semples and the Christian Hierings.

"There were no streets, only the three houses amid the dunes, although a gravel road was in the process of becoming what is now The Boulevard.

"This was finished late in 1909 and became the thoroughfare and entrance to the community other than by boat or train.

"During the late summer of 1911, the Stimus property burned to the ground within 20 minutes and mother and I took up temporary quarters with the Semple family.

"Just previous to the incorporation of the borough and at the age of 14, I left school to work for contractor Clarence Mathis. I became one of the crew of men building Fremont Avenue, which Mr. Hiering was having constructed to permit easier transportation of supplies to and from his beverage business."

Mr. Casler recalled vividly the day the street crew made their gruesome discovery.

Suddenly a cry went up from one of the workmen and all

others stopped and gathered around to see what had prompted his outburst. The poor man was speechless after his first shout and could only stand pointing to the spot in the sandy earth where his shovel had struck home.

There in the excavation was exposed, unmistakeably, a bleached human bone. Carefully, after the initial shock had passed, the men set to work clearing away the sand. And when the task was done their eyes rested on a full skeleton with a shock of red hair still attached to the skull.

The digging had also uncovered bits of rough clothing, bearing all the marks of a sailor's garb. There were a few fragments of rusted metal that appeared to resemble a belt buckle of the type pirates were always pictured as wearing.

Mr. Casler said the work crew was at a loss to decide what should be done with their discovery. It was finally decided to send a messenger to notify officials at the county seat in Toms River. The reply that came back didn't help them in their quandry. The Toms River officials, recommended that because of the obvious age of the skeleton, it simply be reburied.

"At that time," Mr. Casler related, "Clarence Anthony was building a home in this area. He decided that he would re-inter the skeleton in the foundation of his fireplace. As far as is known, the red-haired pirate is still in his resting place, where he was deposited 50 years ago."

The Anthony house is gone but the foundation was never disturbed. It lies in the western section of Carteret Avenue, an area close to where Cranbury Inlet once connected the bay and the ocean.

The stories of the sea and its mysteries would not be complete without recounting the tale of the Disappearing Wreck as told by Mrs. Preston Hibbler, a resident of Seaside Heights throughout its existence, and now 82.

As a young widow, Mrs. Hibbler earned a livelihood for her family of three boys, by serving as cook for the 35-man crew of the Seaside Heights Fisheries operated by Albert Hiering and Anthony Steigerwald.

In her free hours, Martha Hibbler made a practice of walking the beaches with her young brood, partly to help her forget the grief of her recent widowhood. She would pack picnic lunches so that they could spend full, uninterrupted days among the dunes.

It was late in the summer of 1913, and often a heavy fog would roll in from the sea blotting out the view. It was on such a day, she recalls, that she was sitting quietly watching the boys at play on the beach at the foot of Hiering Avenue.

Suddenly the sun burned through the mist and a strange sight greeted her eyes. Framed in the opening in the fog was the remains of a ship not more than 100 feet from the shore. Sitting high on a sandbar, the ribs of the ship showed clearly and coal in the galley was visible to the naked eye. Broken masts and spars were plainly outlined.

Even as she watched, transfixed by the sight, Mrs. Hibbler said, the sunlight dimmed, the fog closed in again and the ship disappeared from view. She summoned other townspeople to tell them of her experience and a watch was set up on the shore. But even in the following days when the fog had lifted there was not a sign of the wreck. It was never seen again.

People of the town could only surmise that following tides had once again condemned the hulk to the depths and with it any clues to its identity, whether it be a trading vessel or pirateer.

There was another era to follow that was to produce some strange occurrences on the beaches about which there was nothing illusory. It was the age of Prohibition and its by-product: rum-running.

It was an exciting day early in December of 1924 when a liquor-laden runner ran afoul of heavy seas and spilled its cargo on the beach near Sheridan Avenue.

Virtually all the townspeople had some part in the excitement but none more prominently than a beachfront cottager who had come to Seaside Heights to spend the Thanksgiving holidays.

Alfred Spahmer had been awakened in the early hours of Saturday morning by voices outside his home. Armed with a revolver he went out to investigate and found a group of men talking excitedly on the beach.

"What's the trouble, boys?" he asked. They replied that while fishing their boat had become disabled and run aground.

Noticing several cases lying about he said: "I suppose these contain salt fish."

The men laughingly said yes, but when they handed him a bottle of liquor Mr. Spahmer knew the right answer.

He was fully convinced when the men offered him a large sum of money to use his private garage as a storage place. When he refused, the rum-runners began burying cases in the sand under the boardwalk and in nearby shrubbery.

But daylight was coming and with it other people from the town. A wild scramble for the cargo began, some men even leaping fully clothed into the bitter cold surf to retrieve the liquor.

Salvagers had a field day, carrying away their precious finds in cars and trucks until police and coast guards could restore order. More than 40 cases of brandy and whisky and the disabled boat were seized by authorities. The rum-running crew had disappeared in the excitement.

14 ◆

Things Just Don't Happen

There is a truism in the fertile field of public relations to the effect that "nothing just happens—somebody's got to make it happen."

No truer appraisal could be made of Seaside Heights' leap to its position in the resort field—especially during the past quarter of a century.

The steady economic growth of the community, the growing numbers of resort visitors and popularity of the resort, sharply reflect the fact that "things have truly been made to happen."

About one mile square, with fewer than 1000 wintertime residents, it vies with its larger resort neighbors of Asbury Park to the north and Atlantic City and Wildwood to the south, as a place which attracts countless thousands of seasonal fun lovers. In recent years it has begun to attract sizeable weekend crowds the year 'round. "See you at Seaside" has become a slogan paying off in patronage.

True, the present day promotions have had their forerunners. An active Board of Trade existed in the Borough from 1920 to 1930. It worked to attract new visitors, new investments and new ratables. It staged quite a few Special Events — the Baby Parades which were promoted around 1927 attracted thousands of spectators and an impressive number of entries.

The Motor Cavalcades which the early-day boosters of the

resort staged throughout New Jersey and the surrounding states, are still talked about. Many of the merchants recall that they contributed merchandise bearing the insignia of Seaside Heights which was distributed in such places as Passaic, Paterson, Princeton, Pottstown and Palmyra.

Beyond all the traditional resort promotion ideas of the past, a steady number of original ones have been dreamed up by the white-thatched Mayor Tunney and his brace of public relations aides, Chief McDevitt and son-in-law Ed Groffie.

Operating on a modest budget of municipal advertising funds, Seaside Heights has invoked in recent years a continuing series of attention-getting ideas. The grey-suited Madison Avenue "public relations" practitioners would command a real high price if they had prescribed them.

It is, for instance, the only resort of any consequence which utilizes the sides of railroad bridges throughout a strategic area on which to emblazon a whole series of large signs calling attention to Seaside Heights, which countless millions of motorists can't miss.

Never one to imitate other resorts, the Mayor foresaw the wide-spread attention which the nation's press and TV would give to such "firsts" as the closed-circuit municipal television system, the initiation of the gold painted, off-shore boat patrol, "Miss Seaside Heights," and a host of special events built around beachfront promotion programs.

Who else would suggest raffling off a regal Rolls Royce on the Boardwalk and get reams of newspaper space, when the best that Atlantic City, Asbury Park or Wildwood organizations could offer were Chevrolets, Fords or Buicks?

Where else would they initiate such attention-getting ideas as a huge 550,000 gallon ball shaped water tank, tinted gold to rival the sun; gold tinted refuse cans for the 50th Anniversary, gold 'phone booths, a municipal flag on gold nylon, which has as its center crest a prancing carousel horse with a face suspiciously reminiscent of its marine relative, the Venetian Sea Horse? Where else would Boro employees wear gold shoes?

Who else could foresee the great amount of newspaper space and TV time to be gotten by merely advancing the idea of building concrete shelters under the Boardwalk which could be profitably used for parking thousands of summertime cars and relieve the traffic problems, while waiting for the Russians to drop the "thing."?

Where else are honored guests given gold toothpicks? Where else would couples celebrating their 50th Wedding Anniversary, and individuals celebrating their 50th Birthday be given Gold Certificates commemorating the fact that Seaside Heights is celebrating its Golden Anniversary in 1963-64? Where else could school kids earning an "A" on their report cards, be rewarded with free rides on the Merry-go-Round and other attractions as a recognition of their scholastic attainments?

But while all of these ideas were rolling up huge volumes of newspaper and magazine space, reflected in the attraction of more people, with more money to spend, the whole idea was being carried out on an extremely limited budget.

"Sure," declares Mayor Tunney, "anybody can spend a lot of the taxpayer's money in running a big advertising campaign —but promoting a resort is no different than a department store. You've got to make every dollar count, if you're going to run a successful operation." And successful it has been!

Seaside Heights is a town for the "average man"—especially the "average working man" and his family interested in fun and relaxation. It makes no pretensions about being another Newport or Palm Beach.

This is best exemplified by the attitude of the wife of an out-of-state banker who accompanied her husband to Seaside Heights where he came to inspect the site of some proposed bond underwritings. "But you seem to get so many working people here," she remarked condescendingly to Mayor Tunney. "That's Right, Madam," he replied, "we get all kinds of people here—we invite them to patronize all of our amusements and attractions and when it is all over, we let the bank *try* to separate the money."

And indeed, as hundreds of businessmen in a large section of surrounding Ocean County, who benefit immeasurably from the influx brought to Seaside Heights, make out their daily deposit slips—it is impossible, for them, or the banks, "to *separate* the money."

15 ◆

Our People

Throughout the pages of this chronicle there have appeared, and reappeared, names of individuals and families who by word or deed have contributed to the story of Seaside Heights' first 50 years.

But no less important are the people of the town who just by their presence and activities on the day-by-day scene give their interest, their faith and their support, to the growth of Seaside Heights.

Mayor Tunney and the Borough Officers have a special tribute for the "people" of their town.

"No one person can claim that he has made the greatest contribution. No one should feel that he has made the smallest! Seaside Heights is the product of all the people! We could accomplish nothing without the support—moral and material—of everyone who calls this community home. We are merely the instruments our people have created, to give action and direction to their hopes, their dreams and desires! Without them we are nothing! Let everyone realize this and take pride in the contribution they have made."

"We want the record to show who these people are." They include "the following and many more, who have lived, worked and visited in our community."

Mrs. Emilie Akrivogianis
Gust Akrivogianis
Mrs. Mary V. Ambrunn
William C. Ambrunn
Mrs. Emma K. Anderson
John F. Anderson
Leslie B. Anderson
Mrs. Lillian W. Anderson
Robert Anderson
Mrs. Mary A. Antonelli
Nicholas Antonelli
Muriel H. Arden
Thomas R. Arden
Bert Avella
Gus Avella
Mrs. Ruth Avella
Mrs. Winnie Avella

Mrs. Harriet Bailey
Mrs. Clara M. Barber
J. Taylor Barber
Carlo C. Barraco
Mrs. Girolema Barraco
Charles J. Barrett
Rev. Thomas T. Barry
George A. Bassinder
Mrs. Ruby Bassinder
Allen E. Beahm
Mrs. Mary Beahm
Mrs. Caroline D. Beale
Mrs. Amelia Becica
Florian J. Beiseigel, Sr.
Mrs. Norma F. Beiseigel
Christopher S. Belamarich, Jr.
Joseph Belinsky
Mrs. Wilma Belinsky
John W. Bellangee
Antonio Bellio
John Bellio
Mrs. Maria Bellio
Mrs. Marie Bellio
Mrs. Emma Bennett
George A. Bennett
Mrs. Katie Bentley
David J. P. Bentz
Madeline H. Bentz
Bernard E. Berger
Anton Beuschl, Jr.
Mrs. Emma Bittel
John R. Bittel
Richard H. Bittel
Mrs. Hazel I. Black
Fred Bliss
C. Thomas Bodine
Claude T. Bodine
Mrs. Elsie C. Bodine
Miss Anna M. Borley

Mrs. Margaret Mary Borton
Mrs. Helen Boyce
Mrs. Evelyn N. Boyd
Mrs. Helen E. Boyd
Hugh J. Boyd, Jr.
James J. Boyd
John J. Boyd
Joseph James Boyd
Mrs. Marelene E. Boyd
Mrs. Rosalie D. Boyd
Mrs. Veronica M. Boyd
Francis E. Brady, Jr.
Charles L. Brinster
Mrs. Madeline E. Brinster
Charles Brown
Christian W. Brown, Jr.
Chris. W. Brown
Mrs. Elizabeth Brown
Mrs. Helen A. Brown
Mrs. Lillian E. Brown
Thomas F. Brown
Mrs. Mildred Brugno
Salvatore Brugno
Mrs. Celestine H. Buckley
Frederick W. Budde
Mrs. Dorothy A. Bunting
Mrs. Florence S. Bunting
William S. Bunting
Mrs. Eileen E. Butler
John J. Byrne
Margaret Byrne

George Cain
Henry Cain
Mrs. Cora M. Callahan
Jack Capizzi
Mrs. Margaret Capizzi
Mrs. Jardean A. Capral
Mrs. Bertha Carr
Cleo T. Carrington
Mrs. Mae E. Carrington
Margaret Carroll
Anthony Carrozza
Mrs. Victoria Carrozza
Alfred Carter
Mrs. Elizabeth Carter
Bessie F. Casler
Mrs. Edna Joan Casler
Miss Mary Casler
Vernon C. Casler
William E. Casler
Miss Virginia Cattanio
John J. Cavanaugh
Mrs. Marion R. Cavanaugh
Robert M. Cavanaugh
Mrs. Alma Chabok
Richard Chabok

Malcolm Ray Chaney
Mrs. Margaret E. Chaney
William C. Chapman
Mrs. Josephine Cheresko
Walter Cheresko
John J. Christian
Mrs. Helen H. Cobb
James Bruce Cobb
James Bruce Cobb, Jr.
Armando Cocci
Mrs. Josephine Marion Cocci
James Colicchio
William J. Connell
Jerry Conners
Charles H. Cook
Mrs. Emily Cook
George F. Cook
Joseph F. Cook
Mrs. Margaret Cosgrove
Richard Cosgrave
Mrs. Anna Coughlin
Joseph T. Coughlin
William C. Covert
Mrs. Claire G. Cowles
Nelson D. Cowles
Mrs. Clare R. Cullen
Mrs. Minnie Culmone
William V. Culmone
Mrs. Florence S. Cummings
Robert F. Cummings
Frank T. Cummings
Mrs. Anna Cunningham
Mrs. Lucy May Cunningham
William C. Cunningham

Antonio Dalesandrino
Mrs. Jennie Dalesandrino
Quenton R. Davenport
Mrs. Thelma Davenport
Joseph DeAngelis
Mrs. Mae DeAngelis
John J. Dee, Jr.
Mrs. Elizabeth Degoda
Max Degoda
Mrs. Laura DeGuglielmo
Mrs. Olive M. DeHorsey
Reed DeHorsey, Jr.
Louis DeJulio
Louis A. de la Parra
Mrs. Ruth de la Parra
Mrs. Angela M. Dell Abadia
John DeMarco
Edward Adelbert DeMott
Mrs. Mabel Viola DeMott
Morton W. DeShay
Mrs. Ruth DeShay
Mrs. Cora W. Detwiler

William J. Dey
Mrs. May Dickson
William J. Dickson
Mrs. Edythe Dillman
John J. DiRienzo
Mrs. Salvina L. DiRienzo
Miss Carol Dirkin
Mrs. Catherine Dirkin
Mrs. Margaret E. Dirkin
William A. Dirkin, Jr.
Charles E. Dishon
Charles V. Dishon
Mrs. Eleanore L. Dishon
Mrs. Rose A. Dishon
Anthony Donato
Mrs. Rose P. Donato
Robert E. Drake
Mrs. Frances Droughman

Mrs. Anna H. Edell
Mrs. Jennie R. Edwards
Luther F. Edwards
George A. Erb
Mrs. Margaret J. Erb
Cornelius C. Evans

Mrs. Helen Fabbri
Louis J. Fabbri
Miss Joan B. Fagan
Mrs. Diane C. Feistel
Frank Feistel
Mrs. Mary A. Feistel
Mrs. Anna Ferguson
Charles J. Ferrara
Mrs. Eleanor M. Ferrara
Mrs. Hazel M. Filippone
John L. Filippone
James Fish
Mrs. Louise Fish
Charles Herman Fleischer
Mrs. Johanna Fogarty
Miss Barbara Foley
Mrs. Marie Foley
Miss Dorothy C. Forrester
Mrs. Mildred L. Frake
Percy L. Frake
Chester A. Franklin
James D. Fraser
Mrs. Miriam E. Fraser
Mrs. Eva Furrer
Philip Furrer

Andrew R. Gabriel
Mrs. Elaine Gabriel
Mrs. Evelyn J. Gabriel
Ward L. Gabriel
Mrs. Delia Gardler

Frank Garofolo
Mrs. Helen Garofolo
Mrs. Ida M. Gaskill
Oscar R. Gaskill
Charles Gawrystak
Mrs. Nellie Gawrystak
Mrs. Alice E. Geiler
Mrs. Jeanette M. Gillies
John Gillies
Mrs. Carol Ann Gilmore
Henry C. Gilmore
Henry C. Gilmore, Jr.
Mrs. Louise K. Gilmore
Mrs. Mary Anna Goehrig
Mrs. Eunice W. Golden
Francis J. Golden
John R. Golden, Sr.
Leopold Golden
Israel Gordon
Mrs. Pauline Gordon
Mrs. Lena D. Gorneman
Paul C. Gorneman
Mrs. Adaline B. Gossweiler
Carl H. Gossweiler
Mrs. Evelyn Graichen
Gerald L. Graichen
Mrs. Joyce Graichen
Edward S. Granger
Mrs. Foy H. Grauf
Henry F. Grauf
Mrs. Annabell Green
George E. Green
Edward F. Groffie
Mrs. Frances Groffie
Mrs. Sandra Groffie
Mrs. Virginia Groffie
Mrs. Amalie Caroline Groper
Miss Helen C. Grover
Mrs. Ethel Gunson

Mrs. Anna R. Haines
Foster R. Haines
Mrs. Anna C. Haley
Daniel B. Haley
Mrs. Leila Hall
Rev. Robert E. Hall
Mrs. Marion Hanley
Robert Hanley
Mrs. Miriam C. Harding
Forrest Hargrove
Mrs. Mary G. Harvey
Mrs. Elsa Hatfield
Frederick A. Hatrak
Mrs. Helen Hatrak
John M. Hatrak
Mrs. Theresa Hatrak
Clarence Hawley

Mrs. Sarah Ann Hawley
Mrs. Florence Heffernan
Martin S. Heffernan
Mrs. Mary Henningsen
Walter Henningsen
Mrs. Kathryn Hershey
Mrs. Mabel A. Hershey
Paul K. Hershey
Paul Kenneth Hershey
Mrs. Elizabeth R. Hess
Joseph F. Hess
Mrs. Edna Hettick
Howard Hettick
Mrs. Florence M. Hewitt
Preston A. Hibbler
J. Himes Townsend
Elizabeth Keresztury Holland
Mrs. Margaret Hopler
Robert B. Hopler
Adelbert T. Hopson
Mrs. Anna Hopson
Mrs. Frances M. Hopson
Mrs. Judith Hopson
Norman W. Hopson
Warren R. Hopson
William A. Hopson
Mrs. Maria Horant
Raymond J. Horant
Mrs. Elizabeth Hornyai
Joseph Hornyai
Mrs. Ida M. Hotaling
Arthur S. Hurley
Mrs. Ethel P. Hurley
Anthony Iannuzzio
Mrs. Carol Iasillo
Robert T. Iasillo
Alexander J. Idzik
Mrs. Carmela Iovine
Mrs. Alma Geraldine Ipri
Mrs. Albina Ipri
Frank Ipri
James C. Ipri
Leonard Ipri
Mrs. Rita R. Ipri
Albert A. Israel

Mrs. Birdie L. Jennings
Fred Jennings
James Robert Johnston
Peter J. Jurczyk
Mrs. Victoria Jurczyk

David Kahn
Marvin E. Kahn
Mrs. Mildred E. Kahn
Mrs. Agnes M. Kaminski
Peter J. Kaminski, Jr.

Robert E. Kaminski
Mrs. Angela Karcich
John Karcich
Mrs. Sara Karge
Mrs. Anna Kaufmann
Mrs. Margaret A. Kauffman
Carles M. Kessler
Mrs. Margaret A. Kessler
Mrs. Doris M. Keyes
Leo Kiernan
Julian George Kilroy, Jr.
Mrs. Mary C. Kinnard
William J. Kinnard
Henry J. Klee
Mrs. Jean F. Klee
Mrs. Phobe M. Kleinback
Roy F. Kling
William G. Knapp
Edward S. Koch
Mrs. Mildred Koch
Russell G. Koch
John Kolaska
Mrs. Mary Kolaska
Joseph Koschek
Mrs. Diana J. Kostiha
Joseph J. Kostiha
Mrs. Mary H. Esher Kramer
Mrs. Lillian Kruta
William Kruta
Nicholas S. Kucharewski
Karl Kunz
Mrs. Rosa Kunz

Mrs. Mae Rose LaCicero
Mrs. Fillomena Lafko
Harry William Lafko
William F. Lafko
James Richard Larkin
Mrs. Mary Faith Larkin
Gerald LaStella
Panfilio LaStella
Phyllis LaStella
Mrs. Doris E. Lawyer
Sandford G. Lawyer
Mrs. Ann Lee
Harold Lee
Mrs. Helen Lee
Henry R. Lee
Albert R. Leedom
Mrs. Lillian C. Leedom
Mrs. Eleanore A. Lees
Irvin E. Lees
Edward R. Lemley
Mrs. Emma F. Lemley
James D. Leonard
Miss Angelina Lepore
James Lepore

Mrs. Mary Lepore
Edwin T. LeQuear
Ethel LeQuear
Mrs. Josephine Licausi
James Liguori
Leona Livingston
Mary Liwacz
Mrs. Gertrude Lockwood
Mrs. Mary Lombardi
Mrs. Frances Lomonico
Joseph S. Lomonico
Angelo Loperfido
Mrs. Margaret B. Loperfido
Frank R. Lord
Mrs. Helen Loundy
Mrs. Nannie Lovell
Seth Lovell
Seth Joseph Lovell, Jr.
Joseph A. Luciano
Mrs. Vivian M. Luciano
Mrs. Josephine Lumi
Louis Lumi
Mrs. Rose Lumi
William Lumi
Mrs. Gladys E. Lutz
John S. Lutz
Edward J. Lyons, Jr.
Bohdan R. Lysak

Mrs. Theresa Macchiarelli
Mrs. Clara N. MacKannon
G. Earle MacKannon
Peter Madia
Harold Manheimer
Mrs. Jean Manheimer
Mrs. Elizabeth Manning
James E. Manning
Gottlob Mannschreck
Mrs. Mary Mannschreck
Clyde G. Marcy
Donard F. Marcy
Francis Marincola
Mrs. Mae Marshall
Joseph Martucci, Jr.
Joseph W. Martucci, III
Mrs. Lucille Martucci
Mrs. Adelaide A. Marvink
Elizabeth Ann Masters
Elizabeth Ryan Masters
John F. Masters
Clyde B. Mayer
Mrs. Edna S. Mayer
Mrs. Helen Mazza
Tony Massa
Mrs. Edna Mazzanti
Mrs. Edythe D. Mazzanti
Guerino N. Mazzanti

Guido Mazzanti
Guido Mazzanti, Jr.
Mrs. Mary L. Meals
Theodore S. Meals
Mrs. Dorothy L. Meder
Mrs. Helen C. Mele
Joseph M. Mele
Edna G. Mellon
Sarah Mentzel
Mrs. Flora Meredith
Robert W. Meredith
Dorothy L. Mesanko
Francis G. Mesanko
Frank Mesanko
Gladys Ceclia Mesanko
Margaret Mesanko
Hertha Mezik
May Michael
Charles R. Mills, Sr.
Ann C. Miskofsky
Agnes Montferrat
William Montferrat
John Moros
Pearl Moros
E. Duane Morse
Stephen Muller
Albert Murphy
Mrs. Anna Murphy
Mrs. Eugenia Murphy
George A. Murphy
James D. Murphy
Sarah Murphy
Mrs. Ruth Murray
Theodore A. Murray
Albert T. Myre
Mrs. Jennie Myre
Charles McAllister
Hazel L. McCann
Ray R. McCann
Margaret H. McClain
Helen W. McConnell
Mrs. Nancy M. McConnell
William J. McCullen, Jr.
Hugh A. McDevitt
Esther V. McDevitt
Rose McDevitt
Margaret Ann McGann
Thomas McGann
Henry P. McGowan
Francis McGrath
Eileen E. McGrath
Lawrence McGrath
Marie McGrath
Joan McKelvey
John P. McKelvey, Jr.
Nellie McKenna
Mary Louise McKeon

Ida Mahon
Raymond D. Nafie
Ruth E. Nafie
Albert I. Nemeth
Lucy Nemeth
Stephen Nemeth
Catherine M. Neumann
Otto J. Neumann
Catherine W. Nevin
Hannah H. Newell
Albert M. Newnam
Mrs. Gaynelle Newnam
Joseph W. Newnam
Marie A. Nicholas
Mrs. Lucille Nicholas
Casper Nicklaus
Mrs. Josephine Nicolosi
James E. Nielsen
Catherine M. Norcross
Milton B. Norcross
Milton J. Norcross, Jr.

Ada M. Oehler
Fred Oehler
Alton A. O'Hare
Mary A. O'Hare
Mrs. Virginia Oliphant
Walter Oliphant
Ella Oliver
Harrison M. Oliver
Angela D. Olson
Edwin L. Olson
Morris John Odbach
Alfred Ormrod
Emmeline Ormrod
Anna Ossi
Jennie Rachael Ossi
Ethel M. Oswald

Andrew Palermo
Anna Palermo
Nicholas Pallotta
Anna M. Palmer
Evelyn Palmer
Connie Tinna Panagiotopoulos
Deno Panagiotopoulos
Edward Paolella
Patricia Paolella
Attilio Parrella
Mary Louisa Parrella
Mary Patterson
William S. Patterson
Mary M. Peterson
Richard E. Peterson
Hilda Piccoli
S. Thomas Piccoli
Josephine Pinelli
Alfonso T. Poane

Mrs. Blanche O. Poane
Mrs. Jennie Poane
Joseph Poane, Jr.
Mrs. Agnes S. Polhemus
Oliver R. Polhemus
William L. Polhemus
Mrs. Nellie Politano
Russell E. Pope
William J. Pope
Eugene B. Potoka
Mrs. Janice L. Potoka
Mrs. Freda Preston
Jack C. Preston
Mrs. Margaret E. Preuster
William Prina
Angeline Rita Procassini
Miss Carol N. Procassini
Miss Mary A. Procassini
Nicholas Procassini
Mrs. Helen W. Purzynski
Leo B. Purzynski, Sr.

Louis Rabkin
George Radovich
Alfred Raniero
Anthony Raniero
Anthony J. Raniero, Jr.
John A. Raniero
Joseph Raniero
Mrs. Lena Raniero
Anthony W. Raymond
Mrs. Mildred Raymond
Miss Jane A. Reed
Mrs. Dorothy Reutter
Mrs. Mabel Reutter
Thomas C. Reutter, Sr.
Thomas R. Reutter
Thomas R. Reutter, Jr.
Anthony J. Ricci
Carmen J. Ricci
Mrs. Joan A. Ricci
Thomas Michael Ricci
Mrs. Vita Ricci
James Ricotta
John Ricotta
Mrs. Barbara Rigg
Roy A. Riso
Mrs. Myra B. Ritchie
George W. Rivers
George Roes
Mrs. Barbara S. Rolle
Fred J. Rolle, Jr.
Mrs. Gertrude E. Rolle
Armaddo Romano
Mrs. Carmela Romano
Mrs. Kathleen Rooney
William F. Rooney

Frederick S. Rose
Judy Rose
Mrs. Hattie S. Rossman
Joseph M. Rusin
Mrs. Mary Rusin
Mrs. Dorothy Russo
Thomas Russo
Mrs. Ann Ryan
Mrs. Elizabeth Ryan
Robert J. Ryan, Sr.

Albert T. Sachtleben
Mrs. Emma Sachtleben
Mrs. Amelia Sansone
Leonard J. Sansone
Howard Walter Sauer
Mrs. Loretta V. Sauer
Joseph J. Sawicki
Mrs. Valeria Sawicki
Mrs. Bertha Scharf
Martin P. Scharf
Ernest Scholer
Mrs. Marie Scholer
Mrs. Ida Schweizer
John H. Schweizer
Mrs. Edith Scott
Harold D. Searles
Ernest A. Seidel
Edward Joseph Sheridan
Albert Sherman
Mrs. Gertrude Sherman
Harold D. Shinn
Mrs. Marjorie V. Shinn
Walter Silcox
Mrs. Lillian Silverstein
Mrs. Louise Simari
William R. Sinclair
Charles M. Sinn
Mrs. Dorothea K. Sinn
Edna Sisk
John Sisk, Sr.
Mrs. Ethel N. Slevin
Joseph B. Slevin
Frank Slohoda
Mrs. Mary Slohoda
Mrs. Elizabeth M. Smith
Henry M. Smith, III
Mrs. Jennie G. Smith
Mrs. Marjorie M. Smith
Robert D. Smith
Theodore J. Smith
Mrs. Anna M. Snively
James E. Snively
Mrs. Frances R. Snow
John C. Snow
Lawrence P. Snow, Jr.
Mrs. Patricia F. Snow

Simeone Sam Soccoli
John Sodl
Mrs. Loretta Sodl
Mrs. Patricia Sommeling
William T. Sommeling
Vincent Sorge
August G. Speier
Ralph N. Speier
Mrs. Ruth Speier
Mrs. Anna M. Spence
Charles W. Spence
Eugene B. Stampora
Mrs. Rose Stavola
William A. Stewart
George W. Stock
Mrs. Marion E. Stock
Ernest H. Stockinger
Joseph Strasser
Mrs. Helen Stroik
Stephen M. Stroik
Charles W. Suhoskey
Mrs. Irma Suhoskey
Miss Bertha Swain
Earl N. Swayze
Mrs. Elaine T. Swayze
Mrs. Margaret N. Swayze
Mrs. Alice E. Sylvester
Thomas H. Sylvester

Mrs. Katherine Talman
Miss Catherine Tamburello
Mrs. Florence Taylor
Joseph A. Tedesco
Mrs. Josephine Tedesco
Santo Tedesco
Mrs. Helen J. Tepper
Walter Tepper
Mrs. Edythe Tilles
Mrs. Mary A. Tindall
Mrs. Marion Tither
William H. Tither
Edwin M. Tiziker
George E. Tompkins
Mrs. Mildred Tompkins
Ralph F. Tompkins
Ralph G. Tompkins
Mrs. Agnes Tozza
Vito Tozza
Mrs. Elsie S. Tracey
L. E. Tracey, Jr.
L. E. Tracey, Sr.
Mrs. Marlene A. Tracey
J. Stanley Tunney
Mrs. Patricia Tunney
W. Patrick Tunney
Charles E. Turbett
Mrs. Esther L. Turnbull

Eugene H. Turnbull
Mrs. Signa Turnbull
William Chester Turnbull
Mrs. Evelyn Twining
Owen D. Twining

Mrs. Elizabeth Ulrich
Miss Lizzie Ulrich

Clarence H. Vandegrift
Mrs. Gladys D. Vandegrift
James V. Van Kirk, Jr.
Mrs. Alice Varuzzo
Nicholas Varuzzo
John Vasselli
Mrs. Lina Vasselli
Mrs. Ethel M. Vennell
John A. Vescovich
John L. Vescovich
Mrs. Rose Vescovich

John Wain
Mrs. Helen Walencikowski
Leo Walencikowski
Mrs. Claire Walker
Francis Arthur Walker
Frank L. Walker
Mrs. Viola Waller
Mrs. Florence C. Waln
Miss Mildred A. Wanner
Mrs. Catherine Watchous
Herburt Watchous
Peter W. Weathers
Mrs. Pansy V. Weigand
Mrs. Johanna Weiland
William E. Weiland
Richard T. Wendel
Mrs. Margaret E. Werner
William F. Werner
Noel E. Whitson, Jr.
Mrs. Margaret C. Wiley
John L. Wilson
Mrs. Catherine M. Wintergust
Edward Wintergust
Gordy M. Wroten
Mrs. Louise Wroten
Miss Henrietta Wurdeman

Mrs. Patricia H. Yaeger
Dr. Robert M. Yaeger
Nicholas Yankow

Mrs. Caroline Zarzecki
Joseph F. Zarzecki
Henry F. Zielinski
Vincent Angelo Zuccala
Mrs. Dorothy Zielinski

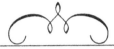

The committee extends grateful acknowledgment

to the

following firms and individuals

BELLE FREEMAN ESTATE
and
RUNDLE & TUNNEY
AMUSEMENTS

OUR LADY OF PERPETUAL HELP
R. C. CHURCH

SEASIDE HEIGHTS, NEW JERSEY

REV. THOMAS T. BARRY, Pastor

THE FIRST NATIONAL BANK
of Toms River, N. J.

40 MAIN STREET, TOMS RIVER, N. J.

Assets Over $75,000,000.00   Trust Funds Over $5,672,000.00

$3\frac{1}{2}\%$ Interest Paid on Savings Accounts

4% Interest Paid on Certificates of Deposit
One Year or Longer

— TEN OFFICES —

BARNEGAT	LAKEHURST
BAYVILLE	LAKEHURST N. A. S.
BRICK TOWN	OCEAN BEACH
FORKED RIVER	SEASIDE HEIGHTS
JACKSON	TOMS RIVER

MEMBER FEDERAL DEPOSIT INSURANCE CORP,
MEMBER FEDERAL RESERVE SYSTEM

International Paint Company, Inc.

NEW YORK • SAN FRANCISCO • NEW ORLEANS

SUPPLIERS of GOLD PAINT
FOR SEASIDE HEIGHTS — 50th ANNIVERSARY

World's Largest Marine Paint Makers

Thomas L. Christian

Insurance Agent and Broker

Licensed Insurance Broker in:

New Jersey	Massachusetts	Florida
Pennsylvania	Delaware	Ohio
New York	Maryland	Illinois
Connecticut		Michigan

3937 Locust Street   Philadelphia 4, Pa.

Telephone: EVergreen   6-2060 (Area 215)

SEASIDE HEIGHTS CASINO

VENICE AMUSEMENT CORPORAT

J. J. FitzGerald, Jr.
President and General Manager

SEASIDE HEIGHTS, NEW JERSEY
SWeetbriar 3-6488

Kenneth Wynne, Jr.
Managing Director

April 24, 1963

Hon. J. Stanley Tunney, Mayor
Borough Hall
Seaside Heights, New Jersey.

My dear Mayor Tunney:

Of Seaside Heights' 50 years of furnishing wholesome and
exciting fun to untold thousands of visitors, we here at
The Casino Amusement complex are proud to have played an
important role for at least half that amount of time.

Seaside Heights has been good to us and, we hope, we have
contributed our share to the widespread fame of this, the
greatest seashore resort of its kind in the world.

Just as the Borough does, we too plan to expand and grow
with the coming years. We have faith in Seaside Heights.

Sincerely,

John J. FitzGerald, Jr.

THE FINEST AND LARGEST AMUSEMENT PIER ON THE JERSEY COAST RESORT AREA

People *and products in stock* *make the difference at* RUMSEY

To serve you better . . . faster! Rumsey's new motor fleet brings you the products you want . . . when you want them. It's another example of Rumsey's continually improving service. So, for quick delivery of your electrical requirements, from a door bell to a complete substation, call Rumsey first . . . simply dial MArket 7-6900.

HOLLY

CHEMICAL

COMPANY

MT. HOLLY, N. J.

Conpliments of

ALFRED PETERSON
Seaside Park, N. J.

Leon H. Wicoff

Seaside Electronic Service

Seaside Park, N. J.

From Your Neighbors in

SEASIDE PARK

All Good Wishes

Mayor JOSEPH J. DELANEY
Councilman GUS DRESSLER
Councilman MICHAEL DUSIK, JR.
Councilman ROBERT P. SUTTON
Councilman MALCOLM FAIRFIELD
Councilman ROBERT B. BENJAMIN
Councilman EDWARD E. PATRICK

COMMUNITY DOG CONTROL

NEPTUNE, N. J.

Compliments of . . .

CONTI ROOFING

122 Sampson Ave. **Seaside Heights**

793-0906

Good Wishes from Your Neighbors in

LAVALLETTE

Mayor JAMES HANKINS

Councilman ROMAN BIRCHLER

Councilman RAYMOND WILLIAMS

Councilman ALAN CONNER

Councilman JAMES BOEKHOLT

Councilman THOMAS ROONEY

Councilman IRA GASKILL

Fred S. Bonderchuk

OUR SINCEREST CONGRATULATIONS TO
BOROUGH OF SEASIDE HEIGHTS
on their
GOLDEN ANNIVERSARY
also to
Mayor J. Stanley Tunney   Chief of Police Joseph P. McDevitt
and Borough Council and Borough Committee

BONDERCHUK CHEVROLET INC.
TRENTON   NEW JERSEY

In memory of my father, Earle Livingston,
who was one of the
early boardwalk businessmen
in Seaside Heights

JACK LIVINGSTON

Compliments of . . .

JACK N. BILL, INC.

and

CASTAWAY'S BAR

SEASIDE HEIGHTS   **NEW JERSEY**

WILLIAMS STATIONERS

"The last word in service and supplies"

OFFICE SUPPLIES

30 WASHINGTON ST.   **TOMS RIVER, NEW JERSEY**

Made in the USA
Las Vegas, NV
11 June 2024